THE BOAT THEY LAUGHED AT

AT

Max Liberson

ISBN: 978-1-4710-4360-4

Friends at Battlesbridge kindly provided directions

Dedicated to my mother Mary.

Contents

Preface

I was lucky enough to be born in Plymouth – a very boaty place. I have spent most of my time messing around on boats in one way or another. In 1976 I embarked on a career as a trawler fisherman, working my way up from 'decky learner' to skipper of a small 50' Scalloper. In 1984 I gave fishing up, moved to London and became a despatch rider. After a boatless period of 8 years I bought a small sailing yacht – a Hurley 20'.

Up until then I had always thought a large diesel engine was necessary for enjoyable progress at sea. My father had been ranting on about sailing for many years, and I began to see his point. The sailing trips became longer and the yachts bigger. My father and stepmother retired from work and fled to sea, ending up in the Caribbean. I read the letters and saw the pictures and knew that someday I too would sail amongst those idyllic islands. My father and stepmother sold their yacht and arrived back at Whitstable after 12 years of sailing about, and not long after that I had a near-death experience, lost my job and was divorced in fairly quick succession. By selling everything I was able to make my dream come true. This book is the story of how it happened.

I hope that this book will spur those on that are considering embarking on a similar journey.

Between adventures I am available for on-board RYA training courses and yacht delivery services. I am contactable via email at maxliberson@yahoo.co.uk.

Chapter 1

The beginning.

7th April 2005.

Midday at Chiswick High Rd, West London.

I tapped the large man on the shoulder, interrupting his current occupation which was hitting the security guard repeatedly on the head while he lay in the road. He turned and looked at me; I could not see his face because he was wearing a full face crash helmet. At first he was somewhat at a loss for words. I asked him, "Just what exactly do you think you are doing?" With this he lost his temper completely and shouted to his mate who was standing behind the security van they were attempting to rob. "Shoot him!" to my surprise and horror, the other man had an automatic pistol in his left hand, he too was wearing a full face crash helmet, I could see his eyes, they were rolling around his face.

The hand that held the pistol was shaking; the first man grew tired of waiting for his mate to actually pull the trigger and shouted again "In the body, shoot him in the body!!" For me time had gone into slow motion, my senses were getting needle sharp, I could see the rifling on the barrel of the pistol, and I could see where the blacking had been worn off by being kept in a waist band, I just knew it was a real weapon, and I knew it was about to go off and a bullet was going to hit me and cause an awful lot of damage, but I also knew that the kid in front of me was almost as scared as I was.

Slowly opening my arms, I took an easy step backwards. "You don't have to do this," I said calmly, and he must have agreed, because he did not pull the trigger. The other guy became really pissed off, and said something I did not hear, and then they ran off. For a while no-one moved, then suddenly people started to come up to me and the guy on the ground, he stood up, apparently un hurt. He talked to the occupant of the van, a lady who was having hysterics, (and not in a good way). Looking down I saw I still had the package I had been trying to deliver; in my hand, so I walked over to the nearby address and had it signed for. Just leaving me with the Winchester document to take there and get signed. This was a rush high priority job, and my controller would be upset about any delay. But I knew the police would want to talk to me.

I walked back across the street to the crime scene, the police had still not shown up, but a nice lady pushed a cup of sweet tea in my hand, I phoned my controller, had a surreal conversation on my mobile phone. "Hi its Max got the Chiswick off but I have been involved in an armed robbery, waiting for the police." "Ok Max let me know if you are going to be much longer and I will get the Winchester taken off you".

I did not want to lose the Winchester wait and return because it was a good paying job, and my controller knew it. I could tell he thought I was telling porky pies, and was just making an excuse to go to a café or something. Reaction was starting to set in and my hand was starting to shake I started to drink the tea, and then the law arrived. Various officers put police tape around lamp-posts and ran about for a while taking statements and a WPC took down my details. While they were talking to the Securicor guard, I managed to slip away.

Back to my motorbike, my legs started to shake; I pulled my helmet on and climbing aboard, hit the starter button and went off to Winchester.

The springtime ride to the old town was a turning point for me, on the one hand I was really elated to still have a pulse, but on the other I felt that my life was just wasting away and I felt like I had to achieve something worthwhile. Life was just too short to fritter away, I needed a proper adventure and right there and then I resolved to always say "yes" to adventure and worry about the details later.

Eventually my controller told Steve, his boss about my problem, Steve made a few enquiries and found out after talking to "Keith" the flying squad officer in charge of the case that I was telling the truth. Keith was a great bloke and told the Steve that I had foiled the robbery and stopped the Securicor guard from getting badly hurt. My name was put forward as a possible for the NCA "Courier of the Year" award 2005 along with some proper hard working Despatch riders. But my real reward was the decision I took that day because it led to the biggest and best adventure of my life so far.

I owned a small yacht in those days, and had just finished a stint at Thurrock Yacht Club as Bosun, and because of that, along with my RYA Offshore Yachtmaster qualification, and the years I had spent as a fisherman, I had been recruited to assist a friend of mine called Martin Knightley and his girlfriend Linda to help them take their yacht to Portugal. Once there they were planning to carry on into the Mediterranean.

The trip would take about three weeks, I was really looking forward to it, not only because I loved sailing, but Martin had agreed to pay me! We were due to leave at the end of May, join the other Thurrock Yacht Club boats as far as Calais Once there we would join in the " Calais Rally", then carry on down the channel, across the Bay of Biscay, down the Spanish coast and from there proceed onto Portugal.

Then I heard that there was a sailathon (like a marathon but with boats) that one of our yachts had agreed to do a leg of but had to drop out of. I was asked and agreed to take the drop outs place, this meant I had to be in Lowestoft on the 19th of June. In order to raise more sponsorship money I agreed not to take an outboard with me and to do the trip single handed as well. The sister company to the one I worked for was run by a keen yachtsman and he agreed to sponsor me if I flew his company's flag emblazoned with "A.S.A.P." and returned with photos.

A week into May I was called in to see Steve. He told me I had been shortlisted for the "Courier of the Year" award and that I would have to attend the awards ceremony at Stationers Hall in London, on the 21st of June. "You will be able to make that won't you?" he asked. "Of course I will" I said, and then wandered away thinking time was going to be tight.

The days flew past then it was time to go, I kissed my wife Rachel and my stepdaughter Marianne goodbye, and joined Martin and Linda's yacht Santolina, at Thurrock Yacht Club. We got it provisioned up and left at the top of the tide for an easy sail down to Queensborough where we stayed for the night. In the early morning we left the mooring before the man who collected the fee was about, and set sail for France. Another yacht from Thurrock, "Clockwise" accompanied us across the Channel to Calais. We had a good sail, and Santolina, a bilge keeled Moody 31 proved herself to be a well sorted yacht.

The Calais rally was well attended; hundreds of yachts from around the Thames area had assembled for a few days. The flat countryside was great for running as well, and I was putting in the miles with some of the others who like that pursuit each morning. One night on the way back to Santolina Martin suggested we have a swift half in the yacht club bar.

There we met Dick Durham the deputy editor of Yachting Monthly. He was with Roy Hart, who is also a bit of a legend in the yachting world, having sailed a Sadler Barracuda almost to the North Pole, and for various escapades in his Ex America's cup yacht called "Victory". I had met Roy several times over the years because he lived in the same village (Battlesbridge) as some of my family, but we had never had a proper chat. Once a few beers had been sunk the night turned into one of those very rare incredibly funny ones that had us all in hysterics.

Dick recounted the story of when his old yacht "Powder Monkey" broke free of her mooring and went off for a sail by herself, and Roy told us about hard sailing in Arctic seas, and racing Victory. And Martin, who is a fabulous mimic, did his impersonation of Hannibal Lector, because he thought Dick bore a striking resemblance to the anti-hero from "Silence of the Lambs". The evening gave way to the morning, the bar staff breathed a sigh of relief when we finally wobbled off to our respected boats. Later on I woke up with a start and thinking a run would clear my aching head I pulled on my shorts and trainers and staggered off. A couple of hundred yards down the road I was sick, and returned to my bunk for the day.

Luckily the wind was blowing hard from the west so I got a chance to recover, before we left a couple of days later. We mostly motored through that day and once the tide started to flow against us, Martin took us into Dieppe for a few hours' sleep. We left at 06.00hrs and carried on towards Le Havre, during this leg a wave swept Martins carbon fibre spinnaker pole over the side, it was a very good "Man Overboard" drill. I took the tiller, Linda spotted and pointed and Martin was able to grab it when we brought it alongside. I think it would have sunk if we had not caught it the first time. It was reassuring that we could work as a team under stress.

That night Martin wanted to go into Le Havre, for a few hours shut eye, as we were heading in there I saw the lights of a dredger go out and a ships navigation lights come on, the vessel turned towards us, I guessed it would get close, so on the VHF I called up Le Havre port control, I was surprised to get a fast answer, I asked them the name of the dredger that had just got underway, they told me its name and I called them up. The dredger also answered immediately and I asked him if he had seen us, he had not, and asked us where we were. "Not far from your starboard bow" I replied and he turned away from us. I was very impressed with their fluency in English, less so with their watch keeping. After a brief stay in the marina we left, and headed off towards Cherbourg; we arrived there that evening and gladly made our way to the showers once we had safely moored up.

I loved Cherbourg. The marina is well sorted, and just outside its gates there is a good park, with a splendid statue of Napoleon on his favourite horse Marengo. If you walk a little further you arrive at the town, its dockside buildings and cobbled streets are wonderfully unspoilt. The port has several docks. The fishing boats moor in the inner basins, there is also an old trawler that is maintained by retired fishermen as a floating museum. There are good restaurants all down the dockside and we ate in several of them, but the best meal we had while we were there was the picnic in the cockpit Linda put together, that marvellous fresh bread, proper butter and an array of cheeses washed down with very good wine, it really cannot be beaten! Refuelling was a problem; we had to do it with 6 gallon containers. Because the fuelling pontoon was out of action

We stayed a couple of days then carried on, past the Channel Islands, we had a good push from the Alderney race, but the fog came down really thickly as we came past Guernsey, fortunately Martin had installed a Radar , and we were able to carry on with a certain amount of confidence. The next day the south west wind came back like it meant it, conditions were too rough for a safe passage of the Bay so we put into L' Aber Wrac'h - a nightmare to enter for the first time. Rocks stick their heads out all over the place and waves smash themselves to white froth against them, a mistake there could very easily be fatal. The answer to safe pilotage is to always know exactly where you are, to have a good hand bearing compass, an up to date chart and be able to use them. We were soon in the small marina, getting cleaned up and then into the nearest restaurant eating a well-earned meal.

L 'Aber Wrac'h is a proper piece of Brittany, the rocks are granite, the tides run hard, the Atlantic Ocean on the doorstep can be a place of nightmares. To wrest a living from that environment the local people had to be tough, they were, and still are. It's a place where anyone who loves boats feels at home and is welcomed, so naturally we loved it. We walked up the steep hill one day and had lunch in the village that lies at the top. On the way back we had to stop and admire an old couple's garden; the colours were vibrant and beautiful, they so obviously spent most of their time attending to the plants together, and looked so happy, I found myself envying their contentment.

We left as soon as the wind dropped down, which was a couple of days later, off Ushant Martin informed me that we were taking in a lot of water. Since "Santolina" has a flattish bottom and not much of a bilge, the pump could not clear all of the water, and there was rather a lot of it sloshing around. This was another chance to earn my fee. Over the years I had been in this position a few times. I knew that leaks are seldom as bad as they first seem, and if everyone keeps calm the situation can usually be sorted. I stayed on the helm and steered while Martin and Linda bailed out by using buckets, that once filled they passed up to me and I emptied over the side.

A small plane came past, and he clocked us bailing out, the plane circled, and then it went over the horizon and waggled its wings. A French coast guard cutter showed up soon after and a man put his binoculars on us, I told Martin to stop bailing for a minute. I gave the coast guard a wave and they reluctantly moved off. I did not want them to get involved, because if we were to be towed in, it would have cost Martin a lot of money. The French rescue service is not free of charge as it is in Britain, and anyway I thought it was important for Martin to find and fix the problem. It was an ideal confidence building exercise. Martin was able to find the source of the leak, it was only a fitting missing from a pipe in the heads. The problem had probably been like it for years but water only came in when "Santolina" was sailing hard on the starboard tack, and it took a period of time for enough water to come in and fill the bilges.

With that scare over we got back on course for La Corunna. Three days later we arrived. We thought we were going to have an easy trip, but the Bay Of Biscay lived up to its reputation with a nasty gale that sprang from nowhere and had us running, at first under bare poles, and then as we were still moving too fast, we had to "reef" the spray hood to get fully under control. The wind blew hard for only a few hours, and the many dolphins we saw later made up for it!

La Corunna was lovely, the first morning we went for a walk and I saw in one bar a waiter tickling the ivories of a baby grand piano. I asked if Martin could have ago, because he had told me once that he was a classically trained pianist. The waiter waved him over, Martin reluctantly began, whining that he was out of practice, and then put on a stunning show that brought the whole street to a standstill. I was gobsmacked! An evening in the tapas bars followed.

I took it easy on the wine that night and the next morning was terrific for a run. It was early and the fishing boats were out in the bay dredging for shell fish with long handled dredges, the bells of the churches where going hard at it, and sounding wonderful. The pavement was wide and well maintained and this helped to make the running easy. Although it was sunny, the temperature was not too hot and my running seemed effortless as I swept past the old Hercula lighthouse that had stood there since Roman times. Then around the outside of the bay, until finally the pavement ran out.

And so I returned, after covering about 12 miles. It was an exquisite run. Later that day we went to a local beach, exposing our white English bodies to the sun. While all around us the office babes on their long lunch breaks, arrived and quickly stripped down to very skimpy bikini bottoms. As we sat there eating ice cream, Linda turned to me and said "I can't believe we are paying you for this!" I had trouble believing my luck too!

Our time at La Corunna was over far too quickly and we moved off to the next stop which was Bayonna. I liked the old streets but in a Tapas bar I ate a bad spicy sausage, and the next day I had a nasty case of the "Trots". It was not bad enough to stop us sailing, but uncomfortable nevertheless. We pushed on to Portugal, and stopped at the first marina. After a night's sleep I got my kit together and we went off to the airport. Time was tight, I had to be aboard and sailing my own boat" Leopard" the next day in order to make Lowestoft by the 18th. Although the flight was full Martin managed to get me on the next one, but it meant getting into Gatwick late at night. I waited, getting more and more nervous, with the frequent trips to the toilet not helping. Martin and Linda said goodbye, and Martin even put a tip in with my pay. I had had a great time and was sorry to go; Martin and Linda are the very best of people, and a pleasure to sail with.

The plane landed at Gatwick and I caught the last train to London, I was able to get from Victoria station to Fenchurch Street Station, just in time to catch the last train to Thurrock. From there I caught a taxi home. Rachel was pleased to see me, but a bit irritated when I left the next morning to sail "Leopard" my Seal 22 to Lowestoft. The tide and wind got us down to the end of the estuary then our progress slowed down as we battled the tide, we made it to Cork sands, this was a good place to anchor and get a bit of kip I thought; not much water around so the big ships would stay away. I hung out a hurricane lamp and tried to sleep, but it was very hot and we were mobbed by hundreds of flies. It was a relief to up anchor and get underway.

We slowly made our way up the Suffolk coast, I was very doubtful that we would arrive in Lowestoft in time to meet the other sailathon boats. But after sailing close to the beach to stay out of the foul tide for several hours, the tide turned for us and we managed to get through the pier heads without hitting anything. The marina was a little more challenging. I pulled the main sail down and came in under just the genoa and then rolled it away to kill the speed, by leaping off just at the right moment, I managed to stop Leopard bashing the pontoons. A Dutch lady helped me get safely moored, and then I went and found the other boats, just as they were going to bed because they had a very early start. I had one of the lads take a photo of me holding up the all-important A.S.A.P. flag (my sponsor's), then I too went to bed.

In the morning I had a good talk with the Dutch lady. We discovered we were heading the same way; she would be stopping at Southwold while I carried on to the Thames Estuary. I could see that the tide would not be good for me until about 14.30, but I was desperate to get back. I had about 70 hours to cover the 100 miles but the weather forecast was for flat calms and very light winds. I left early. The Dutch lady, who was writing a pilot book, chose to stay. Two hours later, after I had struggled to not lose ground against the tide, it dropped off. The Dutch lady came out and found me not very far from Lowestoft's entrance; I had knocked myself out for nothing! We exchanged waves, and then had a good, if slow sail in company to the mouth of Southwold.

She went in but I carried on, finally running out of tide off the nuclear power station. The setting sun bounced its crimson rays off the stainless steel dome, and I was entranced. We stopped making progress when the tide became foul, so we anchored. The following morning as soon as we could we got underway. Our progress was painfully slow but at least I had time to appreciate the wonderful scenery as we went down the Suffolk coast. It took a whole day to get back into the Estuary, then a sea breeze came up and at last we started to move, we pushed on and made Shoebury before the darkness fell and I had to call it a day. I was too tired to keep my eyes open, and the tide was once more against us. I hated to stop because for the first time we had a fair wind, it had turned easterly. All I could do was hope it would still be blowing from that quarter in the morning.

It wasn't! I awoke to a perfect flat calm. We still had to cover 21 miles. The tide started to flow the right way, and in desperation, I got a big oar out and started to row. A light wind filled in from the west and we began to move, tacking all the way we arrived at Thurrock Yacht club at 14.10, and high water was at 14.00. I moored up and rushed back to Rachel, who was at the hairdressers, so I got cleaned up and into a suit, and drove around and waited for her. She was wearing a very bright red dress and had spent a fortune on her hair do. She looked great, so we shot off into London.

At the awards ceremony the place was filled with all the great and good of the despatch world. There we were served a high quality meal, with free champagne. The waiters and waitresses made sure no glasses were empty for long. I stuck to water. Finally the "Despatch rider of the Year" award was announced. Bizarrely there were five of us. We all got it! The other guys did things like never missing a day's work in five years, or riding non-stop through the snow to Scotland to deliver a letter. I felt a little bit like a fraud in their company, but my boss Steve at Reuter Brooks was very pleased. Rachel was a little tired and emotional by then so we left. Later that night I sent a text message to Martin and Linda. "All objectives achieved"! Then I went to bed and slept like a log.

Chapter 2

Due to that award I was able to get more work as a despatch rider and although the sea of east European and Brazilian immigrants were snapping up most motorcycle despatch riders' jobs, I was hired on at "The Doctors Laboratory". The job there involved moving blood and body samples around London. These had a very tight time limit on them, and only motorbikes could move fast enough in the London traffic to deliver them to the Laboratory while they were still fresh enough for testing. Because of the important nature of the work, "TDL" would only employ the best couriers, and the award was my ticket in there.

The work was hard. I would leave my flat in Grays most mornings at about 09.00 and after a whole day of riding fast in heavy traffic I would arrived back home at about 22.00. I was doing five days a week and covering at least 1500 miles in those days. But despite never being late, not taking sporadic days off, and hardly ever crashing I did not get on with the boss. I knew that it was only a matter of time before I would lose my job, so I had a rethink and decided that I would prefer to work in the sailing industry.

Obviously the first step would be to get more RYA qualifications. To that end I went to the Excel Boat show in east London. There I met Edward Brant and enrolled on the RYA cruising instructor course with his school (Downwind Sailing). When I actually did the course it was on the school yacht, a big immaculate old Beneteau called Resolution. The only other student was a man called Edmund Whelan, who had recently retired as the barrister for the RYA; he had held that post for 26 years and was very well known in the yacht world.

The instructor was Adam Smith a man in his twenties, who I came to respect immensely. The first day of the five day course was in the class room. Edmund excelled, I was rubbish. The next morning was the start of the practical part of the course, boat handling. The wind was fresh from the north west and the tide was pushing us onto the pontoon. Obviously Adam would not trust either of us students to extract the unmarked 41 foot Resolution from such a difficult berth… But no, Adam told me to take us out, I think he was surprised that I did it in one go. Adam gave me some more difficult manoeuvres to carry out, which I successfully completed. Finally he asked me about where I had learnt to handle boat like that! I was really happy that I had at last made a favourable impression, so happy in fact that I slipped and fell down the companion way, I landed on the engine box on my lower ribs which made an audible "snap" - the pain was immense.

Adam had seen me fall and came to find out how I was. I was not good; cold sweats and on the verge of passing out. Adam was worried that I would have to bail out which would also mean that Edmund would not be able to carry on his course. I decided to stay on the boat. The next few days were a nightmare, but I completed the course, and Edmund and I became good friends. I did not pass that time, but after an extra day and some revision I did eventually get a pass from Adam. I learnt a lot on that course, and ribs apart enjoyed it.

In 2009 the bankers had crashed the economy, money was getting tight and TDL, the firm I was working for, had to make deep and savage cuts. An east European gentleman would do my job for a lot less than I was being paid, and because of satellite technology the schmuck would probably even be able to find his way around London without my years of knowledge. I was called in and told by the boss's second in command that I was going to get a pay cut, with more to come later. He told me I could accept it "or fuck off". If he had broached the subject in a different manner I might have swallowed the loss of money, but my pride would not let me be spoken to like that.

Ironically a sign had recently appeared on the wall telling us to respect each other! Obviously this did not cover the self-employed riders. I could not bring myself to accept this treatment and I said so, but the rest of the lads grumbled and gave in. I was sent home. The next day I was called in to see the boss, I was expecting to get "chewed out", but instead, he just fired me. Because the boss would not even listen to me I tried to take my complaint to his manager. When I attempted to see his manager I was turned away by her P.A. who was my boss's wife. My boss found out I was trying to see his manager and quickly took my card key away and escorted me off the premises. I rode my motorbike home that day, and realised that 24 years of riding motorbikes for a living had come to an end. It was time to take stock and find a new path.

I owned a nice yacht by then, she was a Trapper 500 called Sarah. I had bought her in instalments off of a nice but very dodgy bloke called "Trevor" who had made a fortune out of running sex phone lines. He had sailed her for a while but got bored and put her on the market, but she did not sell so I made my offer. I told his accountant that someone was buying my current boat "Leopard" for £3000 and I would give him £5000 altogether with the rest over a period of less than a year. His accountant had told Trevor and Trevor had thought it a good idea and was on his way to Thurrock Yacht Club to do the deal. Great, but just about then the guy who was buying my old yacht changed his mind. I called Trevor's accountant but it was too late to stop him coming down.

Trevor walked through the door of the yacht club. I bought him a pint and we sat down, I explained to him the problem and he said" Ok how much do you have in cash?" I said "£2000" He said "give that to me "I did. His next words were a bit worrying "Ok, so now you owe me £11000 how you gonna pay me?" At that time thanks to the "Courier of the Year" award I was making good money so I said £1000 per month?" He said "you can't afford that, make it £600 per month, and if you miss 2 payments the boat reverts back to me". We shook hands on it and he left. It had been a struggle, but I paid off the debt to Trevor and never missed any payments.

I mentioned to his accountant that I thought Trevor was a real diamond. "Yes he is, providing you don't mess him around" he said. I had not heard from Trevor since we shook hands on the deal so I asked his accountant where Trevor was living. The accountant did not know, because Trevor had recently moved. He was able to give me a description of the house and tell me the name of the village. Matters were further complicated by Trevor's habit of changing phone numbers every five minutes.

I managed to locate Trevor's house and he was quite surprised to see me, but invited me in. I met his new wife and even newer baby, and over a cup of tea I told him about the races we had won since I had owned "Sarah". He said he was glad that I had bought the boat and he was pleased to help me because I had been one of the few people to help him when he had first arrived at Thurrock Yacht Club.

Although me and my crew had won a lot of races with Sarah, at 28 foot she too small to live on and as I would soon not be able to pay my rent on the flat I was living in, the flat had to go. Not such a bad thing because it was a horrid place to live and the landlord had recently upped the rent. I was able to move onto an Old Dutch barge; it was cheap because my cousin owns the dockside at Battlesbridge, and the barge was lying there empty. I was still married then, but had been separated for a couple of years. I did, I think, love Rachel but I had found I could not live with her. It had been hard to move out because although I was not the father of her child I had been living with them since she was a baby. We had been on several long sailing cruises together, and although sailing with them was fine, once ashore it all unravelled, and with the added stress of not having any work we drifted further and further apart. But don't get me wrong, I missed them both terribly; it was not a happy time for me. Or for them.

I found some temporary work at Galleons Point marina, but the travelling was costing an arm and a leg and it did not take a great deal of wit to realise that if I lived on a house boat at Galleons Point I would cut out lots of travelling, expensive in both money and time. Looking around the marina there were a few small motor boats that I could possibly live on, along with a Ferro cement schooner that was a real mess. I had a look at her and was initially put off because she was too big - 38 foot on deck and a big old bow sprit.

However I met the owner one day, a small man called "Concrete Ken". He showed me around the schooner and told me it was called "Gloria". I could see he was proud of her, but he had been building her since 1972 and she was far from finished. Many of the things he had done needed to be redone. The coach roof was rotten and leaking. The masts were down and on the dock side. The whole boat smelt badly of mildew and dampness, and there was a massive amount of junk in every corner. The price (£6000) was far too high for me. She was not the boat I was looking for. Over that winter I continued to work at Galleons Point and saw Gloria most days, with her masts out and various tarpaulins draped over her, she looked wide and stumpy.

Months went past. My wife divorced me, I ran the London marathon and sadly Concrete Ken had a heart attack and died.

I didn't win

Chapter 3

Some weeks after poor old Ken's demise, I was having a conversation with a shipwright called Clive who was working on another Ferro cement boat at Galleons Point. The subject of Gloria came up and he said that if I could, I should buy her because she had a really good hull. I said I didn't have £6000, he told me he knew Concrete Ken's son and he wanted to get rid of Gloria A.S.A.P. He advised me to make an offer and I said that if the owner would accept £1500 then I would buy her. Clive was a bit disgusted at how low my offer was and tried to get me to up my bid, but I just did not have the money. Some weeks passed and I forgot about the whole deal, then Clive came and saw me and told me my offer had been accepted. We arranged for the Ken's son Lloyd to come down and collect the money. I went off and fetched the cash. By that weekend I was the new owner of Gloria. And a week later the owners of Galleons Point marina, with incredible timing, found a boat owner who could not afford to pay his mooring fees to take over my duties!!

Having no money, no job, and a large old schooner that needed massive amounts spent on her was less than fun. The first thing was to get her out of Galleons Point so I could stop paying marina fees. If I could get her round to my cousin's place I would save a fortune. Before that could happen I had to put a new coach roof on and things were further complicated because, fed up with being on my own, I had gone on an internet dating site and had gotten loads of responses from lots of women and was going on dates. Why so many women found me attractive I could not fathom, but apparently they did.

Then I met a totally mad one called Helen who lived in Basildon. She was loads of fun and up for anything. I took her sailing on Sarah and she enjoyed it. Then she joined me, Peter Stower and Mad Mick (the dust), on a longish race from Erith out to the end of the Thames estuary, around the buoy that marks the end of the Tongue Spit then back to Queensborough in the Medway. We had a good start and flew the spinnaker most of the way, Helen loved it, I worried that once we rounded the mark she would not be so thrilled. My premonition proved correct. Hard on the wind, bashing into a good force four to five, "Sarah" was leaping about and Helen went down with bad sea sickness. It did not help that she had just had an operation on her foot, not a minor one like I thought, but quite a major one.

She locked herself in the cabin up forward which also had the heads in it. The trouble was all our oilskins were up there too. It started to get very cold and we ended up pleading with her to let us have them. All we got back was shouts of "you bastards!" but she did relent in the end which was just as well. We were lying second at 23.00hrs that night, but in order to finish we had to go into the Medway and up the Swale to cross the line off Queensborough which would mean that because of the tide we would not be able to leave until about 12.00 Hrs. The next day, added to the less than attractive picture, the weather forecast was for strong westerly winds. This would give us another good dose of hard on the wind sailing. I thought that another 18 hours on Sarah could well bring about a total sense of humour loss amongst the crew including Helen, so because I quite liked the woman, and wanted to see her again, I retired us from the race, we took in the Genoa and motor sailed back to Thurrock Yacht Club.

One day I finally I got up the courage enough to tell Helen about Gloria She was very interested in the idea of sailing a large yacht to somewhere nice. I did not tell her just what kind of mess Gloria was in and maybe she thought Gloria was in better shape than she was. I took Helen up to Galleons to view Gloria. It was a hot day; the water had gone green and stank of fish. In fact a few bloated dead ones floated about. At first Helen, who was in a sort of shock, refused to climb aboard Gloria on the basis that she might sink immediately. Gradually I was able to lure her aboard. Then she rolled up her sleeves donned a pair of yellow marigolds and started cleaning the galley, a mammoth task. Result! My major job that day was to get the toilet working. It was a wonderful Baby Blake, but seized solid, I got it out but could not get it working at all, so we drove over to Dauntless and bought a cheapo modern one and fitted it. I promised the Baby Blake I would fix it one day.

The summer of 2010 was on its way out; I was lucky and got some good paying boat delivery work. Helen and I took a sixty foot Dutch barge up to Hull for a man who had just bought it. He knew very little about boats, and was in a bad predicament; his new purchase was taking up a large amount of Brentford marina, and in fact there were only 2 tides per month when she could be eased out of her berth and the lock gates. Bevis the owner drove his smart Mercedes to the car park at Battlesbridge and we all caught the train into London and from there to Brentford. We met his barge for the first time. I realised I should have gone some days before to sort it out. The batteries were flat, the heads smelt bad and the toilet was blocking up. All the navigation lights did not work…. The clock was ticking; there was not a moment to lose. With two emergency jump start packs I borrowed, we managed to get the generator running.

Then once we had a bit of charge in the batteries the main engine fired up. But while in the engine room my foot brushed against the fresh water accumulator and it fell off, a fountain of water erupted. But I was in "full on fix it mode" and I knew that the water system would still work with it taken out of the line, so as the pipe work was all snap on plastic fittings it only took a couple of minutes to bypass it and get on with the next job of sorting the navigation lights. I think Bevis was impressed. Anyway, by the time the tide was up we were in some kind of shape to leave. The next hurdle was getting the barge out of the berth. We had to go astern in a dead straight line, then turn to port and spin it in its own length. There were a lot of posh motor yachts to bash if I screwed it up. Fortunately it all went well, and with the aid of the bow thruster we emerged out into the river.

We had an easy trip down with the tide and anchored for a couple of hours kip off Erith when the flood became too strong to bash against. When the tide changed we carried on, but a fog came in so bad we could not see the bow. I tried the radar but I was not familiar with that set and the compass started to spin like a top as soon as it was powered up! I found shallow water, out of the shipping channel by Lower Hope point. We anchored then called up London VTS on channel 68 to tell them what we were doing. I then sorted out the radar so I could use it. Once I was happy that we could navigate from buoy to buoy I called up London VTS and informed them we were moving and had brought the anchor up. Then we received a call from them saying we were headed for a buoy. I knew that, because with the compass out of operation my plan was to buoy hop. But then a tug lost a 110 foot barge loaded with scaffold materials and London VTS forgot about us.

It became a lovely trip, once the sun burnt the fog away. We were bound for Battlesbridge and the upper reaches of the Crouch were at their best with swans and green fields. The river gets really twisty at the top and you have to know where the deep water is. The channel is not always in the place the charts say it should be. As a result not many people visit Battlesbridge by water. Once we arrived my cousin let me keep Bevis's barge alongside the one I was living on while I sorted out some of the problems while we waited for some fine weather to set in for the open water passage to Hull.

One week later and the weather set fair. A nice big high pressure system settled over Scandinavia. I had my mate Lee Rutter come to help share the steering because Bevis had to go back to work. Helen was aboard for the trip too and it all went well until we were off Cromer. Then suddenly we lost the steering. This was a complete pain, as there was no way of rigging an emergency steering system, I could get her to face the right way using the bow thruster but then the head would fall off after a very short time. I called up the coastguard to arrange a tow into Wells on Sea. They sent the Cromer lifeboat. I phoned up Bevis and told him it was a hydraulic pipe that had failed so he made a few calls and had a man standing by when we arrived to get a new one made up. We were too late to get it that day, but the next afternoon it arrived. Lee had to go back to London, but there was not very far to go to get up to Hull.

Helen was steering as the evening drew in and I turned around to see this huge spider just about to come down from the ceiling and land on her shoulder and if you knew how bad Helen hates spiders you would realise how ugly the situation could have been! I managed to brush it away and out the door before she saw it. The passage plan worked out well and we arrived off the mouth of the Humber an hour or so before the tide started to flood. We had an hour of shut eye before we pulled up the anchor and flew up the river.

Helen was a star and marked the buoys off as they sped past, although I eased the throttle right back so we were only doing a couple of knots through the water. The tide was running at about six knots so we romped up to the marina and then had to wait for the tide to make enough so the lock could open. Once in we got tided up on board I rang Bevis to tell him we were in the marina. He was really pleased that we were there already and drove down to greet us. I showed him over the boat and the repairs I had made. He was very happy that the boat no longer smelt bad and the heads were working properly. He paid me for the trip then took us to the station and bought us our tickets back to Battlesbridge. It was a well-paying job and I had some money to spend on Gloria, but not enough.

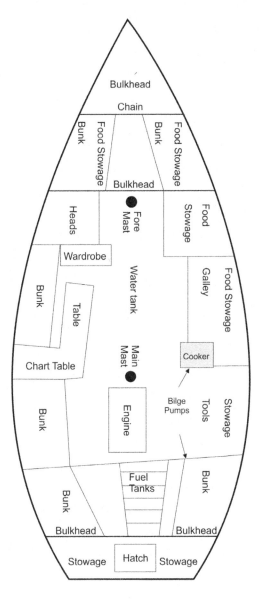

Gloria's interior layout

Chapter 4

The expenses of running Sarah and keeping her competitive were also a big drain. Down at the yacht club a new member had joined. A Peter Stower, who had done the Tongue race with us and was in his later years and had been living in Canada for some time. He had owned a boat like Sarah and raced it on the Great lakes. I was talking to him and he said he was up for any delivery work if I needed crew, and that he was retired and had spare time. It occurred to me then that he might make an ideal sailing partner, if I could get on with him. Funnily enough I received a phone call from Edmund a few days later asking if I could do a rush delivery picking up a brand new Dehler 35, from Pwllheli and take it to the River Hamble. The catch was that it had to be in the Hamble on Thursday morning, exactly a week away.

I had just started a new job, so I phoned my new boss and asked him if I could have the next week off, not exactly the best way to win friends. Reluctantly I was given the week off, so I phoned Peter; he was free and I asked him to sort the train tickets. We would have to leave on Saturday morning. It was all a bit frantic, but the train ride was serene, after changing at Birmingham we boarded a train that took us into Wales and stopped about a million times. Very pretty, but so slow! We arrived at Pwllheli about 16.00, did a shop run while they were still open and then caught a cab to the marina. We climbed on board; a quick check revealed an almost empty Gaz cylinder and no cooking equipment.

A mad dash to the supermarket soon sorted that out. The weather forecast was for brisk easterly winds in a couple of days, so I wanted to get off that night and with a bit of luck we could be there before it really kicked off. While Peter stowed the food and got to grips with a modern boat, I did a rigging check and to my horror I found that the split pin was missing from the bottle screw on the forestay. I managed to get one off of another yacht owner but by then all the shops were now shut. After that we went to a restaurant for dinner. It was a fine evening and after a good meal we returned to the yacht and attempted to get a couple of hours sleep before we had to leave at 23.00.

At the appointed hour we started up the motor, slipped our mooring and left. Once clear of the marina we put the sails up, but had to keep the motor running as there was very little wind. Dawn bought a slight breeze and she was off. I could not get the wheel off Peter, it was sailing at its best, and a huge pod of dolphins joined in the fun. It was hard to be unmoved, as we reeled off the miles past the stunning Welsh and north Devon coast lines. Dawn of the second day found us rounding Lands' End. On the new course the wind came right from ahead so I decided to motor sail, but shortly after starting the motor Peter noticed that the engine was getting hot. I shut it down and did some checks. It was the thermostat, and we had no tools to remove it. So, we had no engine, and no way of charging the battery, so no autopilot.

We steered the best course we could, and by putting in the occasional tack managed to keep heading east. But through the day the wind got lighter and by the evening we were almost becalmed eight miles off of Plymouth. However the forecast and the sky told of a hard wind coming and by midnight we were battling with a near north easterly gale. Our fine yacht seemed to be doing her best to kill us both. The decks had been wax polished and were very slippery. Reefing the big main was a nightmare, with the biggest reef in and the smallest jib set we still had far too much sail up and the boat was almost uncontrollable. We took in the main completely and still the yacht would accelerate up to 8 knots if given half a chance and crash into the large steep waves that had built up, then she would come to a standstill with the whole rig vibrating and whipping about.

All the time the bucking threatened to throw off anyone not hanging on tightly. The only good thing about that leg was the speed we managed to maintain. Over the night we crossed Lyme Bay and made it past Portland Bill. During the next day we got to within 20 miles of the Solent. But I worked out that by the time we reached Hurst the tide would have turned foul for us. There was no way we would be able to make way against wind and tide in the Hurst narrows. Both of us by that time were near the limit of our endurance and I was amazed that Peter was still able to stand as we had not really had any food or drink, let alone sleep for about 24 hours while getting really hammered.

However the wind was good for Portland Harbour and its new marina, and once there we would be able to borrow some tools and take the thermostat out so we could use the engine again. The yacht loved the new course and we made good time and by the evening we were closing with the blessed protective walls of the old harbour. My plan was to sail to the entrance of the marina, drop the jib and motor for a couple of minutes to get into the berth. Just in case there was a problem I checked the anchor was ready to go, as the wind would have us on the beach really quickly if the motor did not fire up.

41

I opened the anchor compartment that was up on the bows and the anchor was clearly attached to the chain and anchor warp. All went according to plan, but then the engine did not start first time, nor did it the second time. There was a pre heat button that had to be pressed and the engine would not start until that had been pressed long enough. The third time it did not start and I asked Peter to get the anchor ready. He dragged it out and discovered the anchor was securely covered in bubble wrap but he had no knife. So he started tearing at the tape with his teeth! Fortunately the engine then did fire, and a few minutes later we were safely tied up. After a sort out we went for showers and a well-earned meal. Then back aboard for a good long sleep. The next morning there was some kind of dinghy racing, or should have been. It was cancelled as the winds were still hitting 30 knots in the gusts. I borrowed some tools and had that old nasty thermostat out in a twinkling of an eye and soon we had a working motor again.

As soon as the time was right to catch the tide right off Hurst we left. The 30 knot winds felt tame compared to what we had become used to, and with the deep reefed main we made good time to the Needles Channel. We took the inside passage and got real close to the beach, then we turned the corner and all hell let loose. I have never seen the Solent like that before. All white, with standing waves about 6 feet high that hurt when you hit them. A text book wind against tide situation. We eased the motor to tick- over revs and motor sailed the twenty miles to the Hamble. At last, on Wednesday night, we tied up in the marina. The brand new boat was a shambles, and both of us were white from head to toe with dried salt. We went and had a welcome shower. Sadly, there were no restaurants open so we had something to eat on board and after putting the heater on full blast to dry out the boat, we flaked out.

06.00 the next morning found us cleaning and stowing franticly. It was Thursday; we kicked the yacht into some kind of order, and then went to breakfast. Getting back afterwards we met Edmund and he helped us do some more cleaning. Then Adam Smith, the instructor we had when Edmund and I did the RYA cruising instructor course, showed up. He looked at the yacht and said "you must have had a hard trip; we heard about that job, I am glad I did not have to do it. Well done on getting here." I had the distinct feeling that we might have impressed him, and that made the whole saga worthwhile!

The owner showed up with the new thermostat and he did an inspection of the yacht. The boat had cleaned up well; no-one would ever have realised what we had gone through to get there on time just by looking at the yacht. I asked him why there was not a split pin in the forestay's bottle screw." Oh we don't use one when we race" was his reply. I tried to explain what a hard trip we'd had, and if I had not noticed its absence, we would have lost the rig, but he did not seem very interested. He paid us, we shook hands then it was time to go. Edmund said he would drive us .We made it as far as the nearest decent eating place. We enjoyed a good lunch and then Edmund drove us to the train station.

I said goodbye to Peter and caught my train back to Basildon. My phone rang and I found myself accepting my next job, a teaching/delivery job from Chichester to Ramsgate. This was a little inconvenient because I was supposed to be riding a motorcycle in London for a despatch firm that I had only managed to work a few days for so far. Luckily the controller there was an old mate of mine called Bill, and after I rang him he told me to take as much time off as I needed as they were not very busy anyway. I had vowed to never go back to despatch riding again, and I should have stuck to that vow because going back was like watching a good friend die of a horrid disease. The rates had gone down to below 15 years previously, but expenses had gone up massively. It was very difficult to make any money, and totally demoralising, so I was glad to get some more Yacht delivery work.

The next job became very weird. I had a couple of days at home with Helen, and then caught a train down to Chichester to meet the new owners of a tatty Westerly Tiger, a small 25 foot sailing cruiser with a fin keel. The new owners showed up. The pair, father and son, were successful builders who wanted to learn to sail the yacht they had bought on an impulse. They both had brand new top of the range Musto ocean sailing suits, worth almost as much as the boat. The only engine was an outboard, with not much petrol.

As soon as we could we came out of the marina at Emsworth. The first stop was to get some more petrol at another Marina. Once fuelled up we headed out to sea, and just made the Looe channel before we slowed up when the tide went against us. The builders were not enjoying themselves and the dad was chucking up, while the son had his mobile permanently glued to his ear. It was quite rolly because the wind was fresh and from the south west. With the coming of evening, I decided that a port was needed. Brighton was the obvious one, and we arrived just as it was getting dark. The entrance can be a bit scary, and it was late night too. The dark walls loomed out as we came closer to them, and our motion in the seas became more apparent, until we reached the sheltered water. We were soon safely moored and I went off to the marina office to get checked in, then I paid a visit to the toilet. When I arrived back at the boat it was in darkness. I phoned the owners, and was told there had been a change of plan. They had gone to a hotel, and would not be continuing! The father asked me what his options were. I said "well you could just leave it here, it will cost you a fortune though, or I could try and get another crew which would take a day or so, or I can sail it to Ramsgate by myself". The builder jumped at the last one. "Would you?" he asked. "Yeah, sure, I will call you when I am approaching Ramsgate". I went back and had a quite meal, then got my head down. After paying for the night I left Brighton in the morning and had a cracking good sail all the way to Dover. I put in there and stayed another night before taking the inside passage to Ramsgate. I really enjoyed that sail, and was sad that the builders had missed it. I am sure they would have been converted to sailing addicts if they had done so. The builder was waiting for me at Ramsgate; I had to get into the inner basin so he climbed aboard for the last couple of hundred yards. He was very pleased to have the yacht in its new berth. Once I had been paid, I headed for the train station, and wondered if I would get another sailing job before I reached home.

Chapter 5

After being paid for that job I had sufficient funds to put the new coach roof on Gloria, which was just as well because winter was coming fast. It was time to phone Karl the chippie otherwise known as "Wonky". He is a big lad with massive hands and if he had a bad temper or was nasty he would be someone to stay a long way away from, but he is one of the kindest hearted people I have ever met. I checked the weather forecast, and it looked like we had a few fine days coming.

I ripped the old coach roof covering off, which was not an easy job to do as it consisted of three layers. The top was chicken wire and concrete, under that there was rotten old vinyl and plywood, and then came the original hardwood skin. It must have looked terrific when the hardwood first went on, but in the thirty odd years it had rotted and leaked and was just a stinking mass of corruption for the most part. Gloria came out of the water by about an inch with that lot off.

I then got Karl down to have a look, obviously the new roof had to go on smartish otherwise the next heavy rain would have flooded out the boat. So he said he would be there the next day and meanwhile I was to order some sheets of exterior plywood from a supplier which I did and the plywood showed up the next day, and so did Karl. A mad day of cutting drilling and gluing and we had the first layer of 12 mm exterior plywood on. The following day the second layer was on and Gloria had a massively strong coach roof. I then went to a fiberglass shop and bought a quantity of epoxy resin and woven glass cloth. It took another two days to epoxy tape the seams, then coat the roof in sections and to stick the glass cloth onto the plywood with epoxy. After that I went over that with more epoxy, the new coach roof was both strong and waterproof; and I was skint again.

Next problem was getting the masts up. I put the word out I needed some rigging and lo and behold, a strange man showed up at Battlesbridge with a trailer full of stainless steel 6mm rigging wire. I swapped a dinghy for it. And my old mate Martin Knightley gave me the old 7mm rigging from his yacht. From eBay I obtained some terminals, and after going down to see Barry at the Dauntless yard on Canvey Island I had a collection of galvanised bottle screws and shackles and was ready for stepping the masts. I waited until there was a good forecast then arranged some of my "big mates" to meet me at Galleons Point marina. Of course the weather forecast was completely wrong and we had a near gale of freezing wind to contend with. The foremast was easy to get up, but the mainmast was a complete bastard. Karl (Wonky) almost got squashed and in the end it was only Barry Spark's superhuman strength that saved the day! It would have been a lot easier with a crane, but also a sight more expensive.

With the masts up and the rigging sorted it was time to get the motor running smoothly. The starter motor was slow to turn over so I took it to a place to have it refurbished. It came back and worked really well for at least twice, then went on strike. I found another one in a locker and tried that, but that one was also dead, so I took them both up to the shop to be fixed. The first one they fixed for free, I did not like the idea of only having one on board so I wanted the other fixed too. But I was informed that the insides were totally burnt out. I was told a new one would cost more than £400!

I told the man to sling it in the skip, and made to leave, but his boss had overheard the conversation and told his staff that if they looked in the old stock they would find one that if dis-assembled could be used to rebuild mine. That's exactly what they did, and so I became the proud owner of a rebuilt starter motor, and a good spare. Another mate found me a bank of nearly new batteries. And another boat owner showed me where the cold start button hides on BMC 3.8 engines. Soon I had an engine that started first go, and ran smoothly. It was time to leave stinky old Galleons Point and get Gloria to her new home in Battlesbridge, with a stop at Thurrock Yacht Club, for a scrub off.

Two friends, "Pigtailed Dave" and "Clever Trevor" volunteered to help me get as far as TYC. They showed up on that chilly March day, there was a lot of cloud that threatened rain, and a wind that was fresh but from the south west the direction was good, the temperature less so. Mud had silted up the entrance to the lock at Galleons, and we were forced to wait until well after half flood tide before the gates were finally opened for us.

Once we were out in the river we stopped the engine and made sail. At first the progress was slow but acceptable, then we got into a wind shadow, and the foul tide stopped us. I restarted the engine and we made progress again, then it quit. I managed to restart it, but I could not get it to run for long. I gave up and we just sailed, or tried to anyway. It became obvious that the hull was very badly fouled. Gloria was being an absolute pig and I began to think I had

49

made a massive mistake in buying her. Progress was very slow, until the tide changed.

I did not want to arrive at Thurrock Yacht Club with a strong ebb tide flowing, but that's exactly what happened. As we approached the first mooring buoys, the wind vanished. I dropped the anchor and the chain rattled out for about thirty seconds, then jammed. My mate's beautifully kept Moody 31 "Santolina" jumped out in front of us and because we hardly had steerage, a collision became unavoidable, but I was able to steer Gloria a small amount to starboard, and when we did hit it was a glancing blow, and by a massive amount of luck some fenders that were hanging off the push pit took the impact!

I passed the helm to Clever Trevor and he steered us past the next yacht while I ran up forward to free the chain. I grabbed the anchor chain and gave it a really hard yank, and it freed off. The chain shot out and because it was off the gypsy, I could not stop it! I stood on it with my boots while it rattled uncontrollably out, and made no difference at all. Just before it reached the bitter end and the short bit of rope that surely would have parted with the strain it jammed again. The foredeck dug down and the chain went bar tight. Gloria span around, leaving us anchored perfectly between the trots. How the hell the anchor windlass was not pulled out of the foredeck I will never know. Once my heart rate had slowed down I made sure we were anchored securely then rowed over to look at the damage we had done to my mate's yacht. I was amazed. After washing off the marks left by the fenders, there was nothing apart from a couple of tiny scratches to be seen. Getting back aboard Gloria, I found a fuel blockage was responsible for the engine stopping; so I cleared it and bled the diesel filters of air and the engine ran again so it was simple to get her on a mooring.

The next day at the top of the tide we got Gloria onto the wall at the yacht club. As the tide dropped down I started to clean off the growth that had accumulated on her in the dock. It was about 4 inches thick and in amongst the weed there were mussels and barnacles, and even the odd rag worm. Gloria's bottom was a complete eco system all by itself! It was a wonder to me she had moved at all.

I had been a member at Thurrock Yacht Club for about 15 years and I knew a lot of people, and over the next few days they all seemed to show up and laugh at poor old Gloria. Most of them had never seen a Ferro boat before because Thurrock Yacht Club has a rule that only yachts of 34 foot or smaller can be on a club mooring, consequently most boats there are made of shiny fiberglass and Gloria stood out like a sore thumb. Comments such as "I know someone with a concrete crusher, if you want to get rid of her" started to grate a tad, and I jokingly announced that I would one day cross the Atlantic in Gloria.

Although Gloria could not stay at TYC I was allowed to place her on a strong mooring while I waited for the tides and wind to become right for the trip out of the Estuary and into the River Crouch and then up to Battlesbridge. There were a few problems. The first was that I could not rely on the engine; the second was that the upper reaches of the Crouch get very shallow, so I would need a spring tide to get up there. I waited at TYC until the weather and tides became good. As one weather system was on its way out the next one was coming in, so the wind was forecasted as going from north west to south, if I could get to the mouth of the Crouch using the north west wind then wait for the south east wind, I would not need the motor.

I left on the top of the midday tide. Gloria, with a clean bottom, was a different boat and was cracking on, so much so that and I realised I would get too far down the Estuary too quickly. So I decided to put into the anchorage at Shellness. This would also allow my father to see Gloria because his flat at Whitstable overlooks this anchorage and with a pair of binoculars he would be able to get a good look at her with the masts up. He had seen her at Galleons Point and had not been very impressed. I hoped his opinion would change slightly. We had a cracking good sail, if a little cold, until I had to start tacking up the channel past Pollard Spit and into the Swale. I started the motor but after a short time we lost drive in ahead. However we did make it into the anchorage and when we were in shallow water I dropped the hook. It was pitch black and I was dead tired and cold. So after making all things secure I grabbed a fast meal and went to bed.

The next leg was complicated because we needed to work our way across the sand banks and the first course was across the tide. Once into the deeper water we needed to claw our way up to get past West Barrow sands, then we could use the tide to run into the West Swin. I found the oil level in the gearbox was low. Topping it up with the small quantity I had on board, had the gearbox working again; I could see no obvious leaks. The forecast was for force 7 south west winds, a bit more than I really wanted. However it was a fine morning and as I was making sail my father phoned and said he could see us and we looked good. Once the main and staysails were set I used the manual windlass to get the anchor up, which was a slow job. With the anchor up and stowed, I raised the jib and bore away out of the Swale. The wind rapidly rose in strength and I put a reef in the main. Gloria galloped along, then disaster. I wanted to avoid the wind farm, and so shaved the middle sand, I shaved it too close, and we slid to a stop. On a falling tide I knew I had very little time. First of all I dropped the main, and it hit the chimney and tore...

Great! I started the motor and gave it a blast of astern and Gloria came off, so we managed to sail through the wind farm to get into deeper water. Without the main sail it was difficult to get Gloria to point into the wind. I hardened up on the starboard sheet winch to try and flatten the jib, but the sheet winch ripped out of the cockpit combing. The jib, released, flogged and joined in the party by ripping at its foot. With just the two staysails and the engine at low revs I managed to get Gloria past the SW Barrow southerly cardinal. At last we could turn north east, and I could stop the engine.

As the tide slackened I dropped the hook in the shallow water by the Maplin buoy. The fuel filter was blocking up and I replaced it with a new one. I bled the engine again then had a meal and grabbed some rest. The next ebb tide took us past the Whittaker and I dropped anchor near the Swallowtail that evening and waited for the morning tide and the promised S.E. wind. I was pleasantly surprised to find the Met man right for once and a sweet breeze wafted us westwards toward our new home berth.

I had just the two staysails up and with the tide we were making 4 knots across the ground, just the right speed to get us to Brandy Hole at the time of high water at Burnham. This would give us the last of the tide to get over the shallows and into Battlesbridge.

However the fickle finger of fate was not quite finished with us yet. I started the engine and when we got to the really wiggly bit, it ran fine for about 15 minutes. Then the drive went again, and we slowed down. While I was messing with it, the keel touched the bottom and we stopped. I put the engine in astern, and was pleased to note we had lots of drive in astern, but the engine began to get hot because the cooling water was no longer circulating. I stopped the engine and put the anchor out, the wind pushed the stern around and we were aground. Again.

A short investigation showed that the engine had moved backwards when I put it in astern, and pulled the drive shaft out of the jabsco pump, I was very short of time because the tide clock was ticking; I got it all back together and started it up. Then the exhaust fell to bits. Fixing that gave us a working engine, in astern, so I hauled the anchor up, backed up to the really tight turn then got her pointed the right way for the final stretch. We made it, and in short order we were safely moored to the dock wall.

Moored up at Battlesbridge

Chapter 6

Edmund had mentioned in the past that he would like to cross the Atlantic again as he had done it once on a very fast yacht a few years before, and although he had a great time, he said he would like to do it slower. I jokingly asked him if he fancied doing it on Gloria and to my astonishment he said "yes" but only if I could get Gloria to Las Palmas in Grand Canaria before the 21st of November 2010. I said I thought that was possible and suggested that he should come up and have a test sail on Gloria. We agreed on the 14th of June.

That gave me four weeks to sort her out a bit. Another period of manic work took place. I also had to raise some funds so I sold a half share in my Trapper 500 to Peter Stower, which was not a thing to be done lightly. Sarah was a yacht I had dreamed of owning for years, but the chance of sailing in the Caribbean was something I had longed to do ever since I listened to my father's stories and read my step mother Ley's book, "Misadventures of a sea Wyfe". On the delivery we had done together Peter had really impressed me and I was very happy to share "Sarah" with him.

Battlesbridge has its own sail loft, so it was a good place to overhaul the sails. I took the main in to Chris Henderson at Blue Marine, where after inspection he condemned as rotten. I asked him to patch it anyway as I had to take Edmund out for a test sail. He reluctantly agreed, and also got me a quote for a new one. I also obtained a quote from Crusader sails. I have always had good service from Crusader and as well as being very competitive with other lofts, all their sails are made in England. They did not let me down; Crusader's price for the sail was slightly less. However it was still of a very good quality and since I was assured it would last a long time I ordered it, and meanwhile for the test sail bent on the old repaired one. Gloria came with a full set of sails, and only the main was worn. The others were usable, apart from the jib I had torn. I had Chris recut the foot of that one so it would clear the pulpit.

The engine was a problem because it was bolted down with little 8mm bolts, just four of them. But there was so little space around it, I realised it would be a major operation to lift it. Instead, to make it secure I used some epoxy concrete filler, blocks of wood and ratchet straps to hold it fast. It worked and the lump stopped moving about. The next big headache was cleaning out the fuel tanks. There were no inspection hatches in either of the forty gallon tanks, so I had to cut into the top of one and clean it out that way. I fitted extra pipes and cocks so I could isolate each tank. I fitted another day tank that gravity fed to the new fuel filters which I also fitted, in an easy to get at place.

I then attempted to do something about the appalling cosmetic problem Gloria had. Firstly I painted the coach roof with cream epoxy paint and then did the decks with blue floor paint. I put in new winches that I received as part payment for another delivery. I needed some wood to mount these on. At the end of the Battlesbridge dock, rotting gently in the reeds was the British Empire, an old Thames barge. My cousin Jim used to own it, and some years ago when it was still in good order, I went to a very memorable party aboard her. Those days are long gone and she is just a shell now, but there was still some good wood on her, and I found some nice bits of pitch pine that I cut and glassed into the cockpit so I could mount my winches.

I told my father about the planned trip. He was worried about it. He and my Ley had spent about twelve years sailing around. They had crossed the Atlantic and had a great time in the Caribbean, but they had also been sunk on a sail from Porto Santos to the Azores, and what made things worse was that the boat that sank under them was made out of Ferro cement! However he agreed to help me and went over Gloria, pointing out potential problems. He was very concerned about the lack of any kind of self-steering.

My father kindly paid for a used autopilot that I obtained from an old pal Russell Cherry. He had a yacht called Morning Song, a beautiful yacht. And that season Morning Song was winning the evening series of races at Thurrock Yacht Club and our yacht Sarah was second. It was starting to look like Russell would win. And then disaster struck, at 05.00 on a summer's morning a passing tug drove into poor old Morning Song, while she was innocently moored up at the club. The damage was so severe that the insurance company wrote her off. Sarah won the evening series that year, not the way I wanted to win the trophy, and despite rumours it is simply not true I bribed the tug crew to fall asleep! Anyway, I knew Russell had a good autopilot that he had no use for. So I made him an offer for it which he accepted. "Pete The Railway" who looks after cousin Jim's machinery made me a lovely fitting to fit the ram into.

And that was how the time went. Edmund came down and we had an overnight trip up to the River Roach. We anchored at the landing steps at Foulness Island, went ashore to the pub, and found it closed. We walked back and had instant curries aboard. In the morning we returned to the Crouch where the tide had started to flood and the wind was easterly. We had to use up a bit of time because we would have arrived far too early at Brandy Hole if we had sailed towards Battlesbridge then, so Edmund pointed her nose into the wind and tide and Gloria astounded both of us by actually making ground to windward!

After a hugely enjoyable sail we arrived back at Gloria's berth and Edmund delivered his verdict. "Okay Gloria is scruffy but looks like she should do the job. Get to the Canaries and I will join you there". He also agreed to help me sail her down to Gosport. September the 6th was agreed. If I thought the last few months had been frantic what followed was, almost panic. A million things needed doing. The barge I was living on would have to be given back and all my stuff stored. Helen wanted to keep the barge on, and then I was asked if I would rent it to a couple of guys who were working nearby for a couple of months. This seemed like a good solution and I wrote my landlord a letter explaining everything. Getting no reply we carried on with the arrangements.

The new mainsail arrived from Crusader sails. I put it on but did not have a chance to use it. It fitted and looked very good. The big jib I had recut by Chris also fitted beautifully. We had at least a full wardrobe of good sails to go with. I did a shop in the local cash and carry, buying food in bulk kept the prices down. I bought enough to feed one person for a whole year, figuring that this much would keep a crew of three for four months. As well as a crate of tinned stewing steak, a crate of chicken curry, two big bags of bread mix, 100 servings of rice, a large tub of minestrone soup, big bags of pasta, several packs of oats. I also bought large bags of lentils, barley, chickpeas, and kidney beans. I bought lots of other stuff to eat and filled several lockers with it. Cooking gas was the next problem. I had a couple of 7kg Calor bottles and I had them filled. I also had a full Gaz bottle. With this lot and 30 gallons of diesel on board I thought we had enough to at least get to Gosport. The date for our first leg departure rapidly arrived.

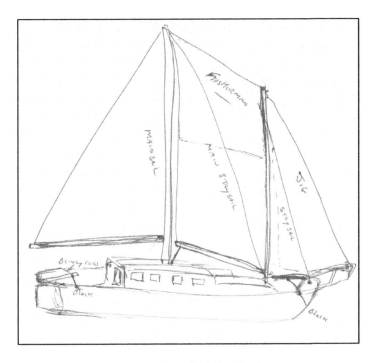

Gloria's full sail plan

Chapter 7

The 6th September 2010 dawned and found Gloria in her snug berth at Battlesbridge. The forecast was not good. A new depression was coming in, first of all we would get S.E. winds, and then overnight cold rain, then it would veer to SW, terrific, head winds all the way, with added rain! Edmund had arrived late the night before with another crew member called Chris, who needed to get some extra miles so he could take his Yachtmaster exam. They had been on a sail training trip and had not had a lot of sleep. If it had been possible I would have postponed the trip for a couple of days, but we only had a narrow tide window to get out of Battlesbridge, we made ready, but with an hour to go and the water was hardly even up to Gloria's keel.

Ed asked me if I had worked out the tides correctly, I was getting very twitchy, a small crowd of well wishes including my mother, my aunt, uncle and cousin, and of course Helen had assembled to wave us off, it would have been very embarrassing if we had not floated. Chris the sail maker had put up a sign with an arrow on his sail loft, pointing out the way to the Caribbean, very helpful! Gloria floated at the appointed time, thankfully, we soon had her turned around and we were off!

Gloria crept past the shallow twisty bits of the river Crouch, slowed down by the stiff easterly wind. Once down to Brandy hole I breathed a sigh of relief because we were in deeper water. The rain started and became heavier. As the head wind strengthened it looked like it was going to be an awful night for threading the complicated sands of the Thames estuary. I decided that a good night's sleep in a safe anchorage would be a more seaman like alternative. So we went into the Roach and put the hook down in good holding mud in the lee of Foulness Island.

The next morning broke upon a different world, the sun shone and the sky was blue, after a good breakfast we got underway and caught the tide out of the Roach and the Crouch. The sails gave us a bit of drive but we needed the engine to make a good speed. Once out past the Whittaker, we turned to starboard and worked past the Maplin sands until we could turn and get through the gap in the Barrow sands, eventually we made it through the Edinburgh Gap, and past the Tongue and Margate sands. I was glad we had not tried that route during the night.

The day went and evening found us off Ramsgate, we went inside the Goodwin sands and carried our tide all the way until off Dover, I called up Dover port control and advised them we were passing under sail, expecting them to tell me if they wanted me to change course for any of the ferry's that enter and exit Dover. Not a peep from them, but a ferry was getting very close. It was my watch and I chose to tack around and reverse our course so that the ferry knew we would not be a danger to them. Edmund thought merely slowing down would have been enough. I knew I had annoyed him because he went down and made a cup of tea. I soon realised this was Edmund's very English way of showing displeasure.

The tide set against us, and our speed across the ground dramatically slowed. We had the engine on and kept it on to motor sail as we rounded the head lands of Dungeness and Beachy Head. The next afternoon off Brighton the engine died. I switched the fuel filters and turned on the cock to the small gravity tank. It certainly made bleeding the filter a lot easier. And in short order the engine was running again. I wanted to get some more diesel so we went into Brighton and filled up one of the tanks. Edmund very nicely paid for it. Once more underway we had dinner, Edmund said it was the first time he had ever been able to sit at a table and eat down below while motor sailing into a force four head wind. I could see his point; Gloria was wonderfully stable and had a lovely motion.

We made Gosport at day break, and I had us nicely stuck in the mud by Hardway Sailing club an hour later! Edmund went and made another cup of tea, while we waited for the tide to float us off. Then we anchored nearby. I rowed Chris ashore after breakfast and signed off his log book. I noticed then that the inflatable was really hard work to row. Later that morning the tide rose enough for Gloria to get alongside Hardways pontoon. Then Edmund and I retired to the pub to wait for Helen. She had agreed to drive Edmund's car down for him. She showed up and we had lunch. Edmund went home and Helen and I went back to Gloria.

Edmund came around the next day with some goodies from the back of his garage including a spare anchor, safety gear, an outboard motor, deck fittings, fuel cans and some lengths of rope. There was a spare anchor, and some lengths of rope. He then drove us over to a chandlery and bought pilot books and charts for the trip. Then we went over to his X yacht and I donned a wet suit and cleaned her off, Edmunds's wife was racing her the next day, and she had to have a spotless bottom.

After we used the outboard, we took it off the dinghy and put it in the car. Ed drove us back to Hardway and we put the outboard and the charts and pilot books on board Gloria. The next day me and Helen put Gloria on the scrubbing posts at Hardway and cleaned her off, the next morning I antifouled her. The only problem was getting her to lean against the posts, she would until the water went down, then she would insist on standing up straight on her broad flat keel. Once all the work was done we went back onto the pontoon mooring.

Hardway Sailing Club was the best place we could have gone to. I was expecting to have to go down to Plymouth to find a place cheap enough for me to be able to afford to stay and do all the preparation work to get Gloria ready for an open sea voyage. I did not know about Hardway, but Edmund did. In many ways this club reminded me of my own club, Thurrock; prices were kept down by all the club members pitching in. The wonderful thing about clubs like these is that they extend their hospitality to visiting yachts. They do exactly what sailing clubs should be doing, i.e. promoting sailing in the local area. It was a pleasure to stay there and I looked forward to visiting again.

Helen had run out of time and had to go back. I was very sad when she went as it would be some weeks before I would see her again. I wanted to do the next leg singlehanded as Gloria had still not been tested in rough weather. My gut instinct was that she would have no problems, however considering that she was nearly forty years old and had never been in any serious weather, she needed a proper sea trial, but if she did have any big problems I did not want anyone else put into danger.

 The weather was not looking good for the next few days; the forecast was for S.W. gales. And we got them; I went on a visit to the explosives museum and did some more food shopping. Eventually I was too bored to stay, so I left for the Isle of Wight.

A nice clean hull after a good scrub

Chapter 8

It was surprisingly lumpy in the Solent and until we got into the lee of Osborne Bay, Gloria was struggling to make any way at all. Due to a blockage in the weed trap, if I ran the engine at anything more than a fast tick over, the temperature started to rise into the danger area. I was too busy to leave the helm and fix it, hence our slow progress. Once in the Medina River I headed for the Folly Inn moorings.

A very good mate of mine called Chris Lewis was berthing master there. I moored up on a pontoon in the river and went to see him later that day. He and his girl Cathy had brought their yacht over from the Bahamas the year before; they delighted in telling me how bad the weather had been and the amount of damage they took getting back. Chris also insisted that I take an E.P.I.R.B he had in his garage and an American gas bottle. Also he lent me some charts. A day later the weather broke and early in the morning I left, Chris and Cathy waved me goodbye. I got a few hundred yards and I saw a boat very similar to Gloria, I went astern, and got a camera out to take a photo, a lady appeared and also took a photo of us, we said our good mornings, a man appeared and we had a hurried conversation.

Then I got underway and made it to the fuel berth. I was however too early. The fuel was not dispensed until 10.00, while I was waiting the people on the boat I saw came up and stopped for a cup of tea. Their boat was called Talisman, and it was built in Fambridge, it seems that she might well have been built by the same man who built Gloria for concrete Ken. The names of my new friends were Simon and Anita. Their boat was quite a bit bigger than Gloria, but they had paid a lot for her and had been refurbishing her ever since. They had to go to work, and as the fuel man eventually turned up we said goodbye.

Once dieseled up I headed down the Solent, and out to sea. The day was a sweet one, and for a short time I thought we would have a good sail, sadly the time we had lost waiting for the fuel man to show up was important. We lost the tide off Hurst Point and so progress began to get slow, and of course the wind dropped off, so I had to start the engine again. With the autopilot steering at least I was able to get a bite to eat. The wind was fitful for the next 24 hours. But then finally we got a breeze we could sail on. Gloria began to move, my passage plan called for a stop at L' Aber Wrac'h, but I could not bring myself go in there. Gloria was going so well!

Alas, the tide turned foul and our progress became zilch, and then with the wind and the tide against us, we began to lose ground. And be pushed north east, what was more worrying was later that night if we did not get away from Ushant, with the next fair tide, we could well be in in the same position the next day. If so I would have become exhausted. Never the less, it was a good opportunity to test Gloria's rig, if anything went wrong the English coast was under my lee, so when the wind freshen I left the full sail plan up barring the fisherman sail.

The wind piped up to about a force seven. I left the full main, mainstay-sail, staysail and number 1 jib up, as we crashed through the big waves. I was glad to note that the   masts stayed up, despite the severe mistreatment, but I'd had enough by midnight and made for Ushant itself, my pilot book showed some possible anchorages, there was no moon, and it was pitch black getting close to the razor sharp rocks that reared out of the sea took all my nerve. The first two bays I tried had too much swell coming in to be comfortable. The last one had mooring buoys and a small village. The hook went down with a splash, and I very gratefully went to bed.

In the morning I found we had a few boats as company. Rowing ashore showed me that the village was tiny. It did however have a good café. I went there to drink coffee. The wind was light and there seemed no point in sailing so I went looking for someplace where I could fill a can of diesel. Edmund had put a shopping trolley on board despite my micky taking regarding it. I had used it several times and on the Island it became indispensable because I was able to bungee strap the 6 gallon container to it, and after rowing ashore I started the long walk across the Island to the petrol station. Ushant is a pleasant Island, and it was nice strolling through the lanes. I had a shock when I paid for the fuel, it coat 30 euros for 16 litres. Glad I did not need to fill my tanks. On the way back I was invited over for a drink on another yacht, some good people on a UFO 34 called Quicksilver, who were on their way to the Med. The skipper warned me that the weather was going to get very bad in Biscay in a few days. I said I was leaving at first light. They came aboard Gloria later and we had a few beers.

An apparently uninteresting view

Chapter 9

As the light came I started getting Gloria ready for sea, the forecast being for westerly winds, just right. The large beautiful white Topsail schooner that had come in the night before and picked up a mooring was getting ready to leave as well. Gloria and I made our departure and clearing the harbour, turned south. The tide was running hard and I was very glad of the engine that was stopping us being swept over the reefs. A RIB with two anglers in it, who were fishing for bass, kept going over the surging reef, then motoring back to do it again. It was a brilliant morning and the wind rose enough to allow Gloria to sail, so I turned off the engine and we sailed. I put Pavarotti on the CD player and the music turned a brilliant morning into pure magic.

I saw the topmasts of the other schooner sailing round the island from the other side. The tide gave wings to Gloria's keel and we quickly left Ushant behind. Once balanced, I did not need to steer. Some dolphins showed up and I watched them from the bowsprit. Later on the wind went more southerly and the tide turned and progress dropped to zero miles. After a day of slopping around I reluctantly started up the engine. Another 70 miles and we found some wind. I put Gloria hard on it and she was off! Surging up big waves and crashing away to windward. To keep Gloria balanced I put four rolls in the main sail, but as I was doing this the pin to the goose neck fell out. I had an interesting few minutes while I balanced on the coach roof trying not to fall off and control the boom at the same time. Fortunately I was able to wrap a halyard around it and then find the pin and replace it.

I noticed that sea water made its way past the fore hatch and I had to strip all the bedding from the fore cabin to stop it getting wet. When waves smashed into the windows, water came past the seals as well, so more stuff was moved. In the end I found a dry place to rest in between keeping a look out. My other duties also included a hourly turn at the pumps as significant water was finding its way into the bilges. As I began to dwell on the definition of "sinking" rather than "leaking" I came to the conclusion that if I only had to pump for 10 minutes in every hour it was only "leaking". I had a good look but I could not find any place where water was coming in from under the waterline, so I assumed it was just the sea finding its way in from deck leaks.

However, I could put up with it because Gloria was making 6 -7 knots in the right direction! 36 hours of this brought us to within 50 miles of the Spanish coast. Sadly that blistering progress did not last and the wind dropped off and went northerly. I attempted to get Gloria to steer using the autopilot but the leisure batteries did not have enough life in them, so I had to start the engine to charge them. When I started the engine the belt that drove the alternator slipped really badly. I attempted to tighten it and found that the adjustment could not be fully used. Then I noticed that the autopilot's plinth had worked loose. In the big swell that was running the autopilot could not cope. I also noticed that the forestay was slack and it was time to seek the nearest haven with my sick engine and floppy masts. The nearest downwind harbour was De Cedeira. I made for it but the tide was against us and we did not reach the approaches until the light was gone. We crept in and found space to anchor close to a moored fishing boat. Once I had lit the hurricane lamp that I used as an anchor light, I was very glad to get my head down.

The next morning the sun was shining, and although I had lots of work to do on Gloria, I could not resist getting the inflatable over the side, rowing ashore and walking into town. It was Sunday and for some reason various ordinance (posh for canon) was being fired off. It was interesting, but as I could not find out the reason for all the noise I went back to Gloria.

I started looking at why the rigging had gone slack. The problem was not hard to find. Up the foremast the triatic stay (the bit of rigging from the top of the mainmast to the top of the foremast) was shackled into a fitting. This fitting had bent upwards, pulled out of the mast and in so doing the stay had become slack. This was a tad galling because my father had noticed the fitting and told me to change it or I would have problems. Still, first thing was to get up and have a look. I decided to commence the inspection in the morning. So I cooked a big dinner and went to bed.

First thing in the morning I hoisted up the top block of my block and tackle mast climbing gear to the top of the foremast. Then I attached my boson's chair to the lower block. I then hoisted myself up to the top and carefully made the end off. A thorough inspection showed that although the after tang had pulled out from the mast, the fitting was not likely to come off because the mast head shroud tangs were welded to it and through bolted, so the fix was to shorten the triatic stay. The only trouble was, that meant four trips up and down the masts. The job took all day, and by the end my arms were just about falling off. Still, at least I had entertained the local fishermen, but they did slow down as they passed, and the wakes that their fishing boats threw up did not knock me off the mast.

Once the slack forestay was sorted I turned my attention to the engine. The belt that turned the alternator was slack and it had run out of adjustment, but there were two spares. Attempting to fit them I discovered that both were too big. I went ashore with a Spanish phrase book which had been given to me by my step mother Ley. It was a special one, in that it had been written for cruising people and was very useful because it had sections on engine repairs. I took it with me along with the old belt.

There was a small shop that did engine repairs on the fishing boats. The man who ran it spoke no English. I spoke no Spanish, but with the book I was able to make myself understood, and he took me to a big store room stuffed with fan belts. We went through them and found one he thought would fit. I took it back and tried to fit it. It was too tight so I returned to the shop. I saw the man and we went back to the store room, waded through the black mass and found another one slightly bigger. I was struck by the patience and friendliness of the man and I wished I could speak the language. I could manage "gracias senor" but it seemed inadequate.

 The new belt fitted, so I went back and got another one and some fuel filters as well. A new filter in the fuel line was needed as the old one was pretty mucky. I decided that most of the water that had been coming in had been getting down the hawse pipes , so I thought that in future bad weather I would stuff them with rags and then I would not have to pump so much.

We were soon ready for sea. Helen was going to arrive in 10 days and I knew that if I went into Corunna I would probably have to stay

76

at the marina, and for that I would have to pay. The place I was anchored at was free, so every day I could stay there saved me money. But then I got a weather forecast. A big gale was coming, but there was still time to get to Corunna. I was worried that if I delayed and the weather closed in, I would not be there when Helen arrived. So next morning I got underway for Corunna. There was no wind at all and we had to motor the whole way with a big swell and sunshine. The fantastic scenery made up for the tedious noise of the donk. Gloria and I made Corunna, and as we approached the new marina I saw a possible anchorage. There was an old fort sticking out of the shoreline and in the lee of that fort there were some moored yachts, and a space where I could anchor.

There was an anchorage marked in the pilot book, but that was further out in the bay and it would be very open to the strong SW winds that were forecast. It took some time to get in and I anchored just in the right place. Then a man came out of the marina in a dory and said I could not anchor there. I told him my problem, so he said I could come into the marina. I asked him the price, and it was too much, so we haggled. To my surprise he dropped it by 50 per cent! Later I found out that the summer season finished on the last day of September, and then the price for marina berths halved. Happily I had arrived on the 30th. But anyway it was a good deal and soon we were safely berthed and connected to the electric.

Chapter 10

The next day it blew hard. Very hard. And it rained. In between parting mooring ropes because of the swell, I made friends with another Brit called Allan Rees who had sailed over in a Hunter Europa, a tiny boat, he had wanted to sail to America but his self-steering did not work and he had diverted to Corunna arriving after 14 days. I think the other marina inhabitants had trouble deciding who was madder - me with my really scruffy Ferro boat or Allan with his dinky yacht.

The showers were really excellent, and I enjoyed the luxury of abundant hot water. A couple of days later I saw Allan standing by the cash point machine with a look of horror on his face, "what's up mate" I asked, " it just ate my card" he said. It turned out that he only ever took out small amounts when he needed it, so now he had no money and no card! I lent him £100, he said" but you don't even know me or my address or anything" I told him it was okay, I trusted him. And it was, as he put the money back into my account as soon as he arrived back in England some weeks later.

Just after the really bad gale a Farr 65 yacht came in, I recognised it as one of the ones On Deck (a Solent sailing school) use, I knew that Edmund had been working as mate on one of those so I went over for a chat with the skipper. He was called Peter, and that yacht was the very same one that Edmund had been mate of some weeks before. While we were chatting I told Peter of our plans, he looked at Gloria, and I could see by his expression he thought I was nuts, this egged me on so I told him I had only paid £1500 for Gloria, his crew, all who had paid a large fee to sail from the Solent to Corunna did not know what to think, the conversation was going nowhere fast, I think the problem was a clash of realities.

On the 6th of September Helen flew in, I almost blew it. I asked directions to the airport at the marina office, it was not far. But then I checked the text message she sent me, she was coming into another airport! I just had time to catch a coach to Santiago and then catch another to the airport there. It was so good to see her. Our first night was great fun, we went into town and ate at the tapas bars; it's a great way of eating and learning the language, we took phrase books and attempted to work out what the food was! The weather remained horrid and windy for the next few days. I wanted calm conditions for Helen's first foreign sailing experience. We got them at last and on 9th of September we left.

Trouble was there was not a lot of wind, after a couple of hours of 2 knots I was forced into to starting up the motor. We struggled on but as the evening came the sky clouded over and it started to rain. The harbour of Lexas was close by so we went in and anchored. It blew up that night and got cold and rainy, so we stayed another day. It was not easy to get ashore and we remained on the boat. The next morning the sun was out again and a bit of wind was blowing so we left. The wind became stronger and we had a good sail to Finistere where we motored in and put the hook down close to a beach.

There was another yacht already anchored, a Canadian boat, I had anchored a bit close but I guessed it would be okay. I waved to the other yacht, but got no response so I presumed they were happy. During the night it blew really hard, we did not drag, but sometime during the night, the Canadian yacht got underway, and left. I don't know if he felt unsafe because we were so close. The next morning we were surrounded by small fishing boats and it was flat calm. A little breeze enabled us to sail off and I was glad not to have marred such a wonderful morning. The dramatic scenery slowly dropped away and we made a few miles before I got fed up and started the engine again. We motored on and during the next night even managed to sail a bit.

Or next stop was on the Island called Ill Cies that was also a nature reserve. We got in late and dropped our hook close to another bunch of yachts. In the morning I realised we had anchored quite close to the very same Canadian yacht we had anchored close to a couple of days ago! We waved, the skipper did not wave back, and soon left. Helen wanted to go ashore, so we did. She got a bit wet in the surf, and we carried the inflatable up out of the tides range and went for a walk. It was a pristine Island, unspoilt with a wonderful beach. We could have stayed there forever it would have made a good deserted island hideaway, if it had been deserted, which it wasn't. Later that day we got underway for Bayonna, it was only a few miles and did not take long.

We arrived in the marina and got tided up. Then we went into the marina office and asked the rates. We got a shock - it was 33 euros per night. I like Bayonna and I wanted to stay there a few nights, but at those prices we could not afford to. The lady would not haggle, so we paid for one night, did some food shopping and then departed the next day. A familiar story was playing out; it was a beautiful day, but not enough wind to sail, so we had to motor.

Soon we left Spanish waters and entered Portugal. We hoisted the courtesy flag Helen had made, because I refused to pay 13 euros for the scrap of printed material I was offered in the Chandlery at Corunna. As the light faded the wind came up. I was really glad because we were seeing lots and lots of fishing gear and if we did hit some I would rather do it without the prop spinning. It was amazing the amount fishing buoys that were in the water, I saw one set too late and we went between the bam boo flag and the float, but somehow it did not catch up on the skeg. I think we were going too fast.

After a night of this I was knackered. A port was needed, and we were close to Oporto so we went into there. It was blowing pretty hard by then, and I radioed up and was given a pontoon number in the marina. As we entered I realised it was going to be a tight fit. We would only get one shot to get in, because if we went broadside to the wind at slow speed we would lose control and bash other boats. Luckily the berthing master was on the pontoon waiting for us, I turned too soon and went astern hard to stop from bashing the pontoon, I think he had seen this problem before, and his fast action in grabbing the bowsprit and pushing the bow off rescued the situation.

We went into the marina office checked in and paid for a couple of days. We then went back on board and soon after a small group of customs officers and a dog came on board. They conducted quite a thorough search. Then they left, five minutes later they were back, the woman in charge said "I am not satisfied, we are going to search some more". And they did, more and more customs came on board, and three police officers. "How can you afford to go sailing" the boss lady wanted to know, "why do you carry so much food, diesel and coffee". I tried to explain that by carrying so much food we did not need to buy so much, and I was not spending very much money at all. But she just seemed to think because the boat was scruffy we were up to no good.

Finally she declared she wanted to see inside the water tank. I showed her where it was, under the saloon sole, it had two inspection hatches, ringed with about thirty machine screws. There was about eight people looking by then, it was getting very crowded. I produced my battery drill. "Which one?" I asked - she picked the forward one. I carefully cleaned it off, and unscrewed the screws, then carefully prised it open. Nothing there of course, "you can put it back now" she grandly announced, "No I can't. First I have to scrape off the old sealer, then I have to reseal it, it's going to take a while". Her boss was there by then and I think she was getting a bit embarrassed, so they left. Helen asked "What was that about?" I replied "I don't know" she went off to fill out our log book and ended her page with the statement, "Gloria is a customs magnet babe".

We went off to find a full Gaz bottle. An expat on the next boat drove me around to get one, but the shop was closed. Still, he showed us a good place to eat, adorned with old photos of fishing boats. We went there that night and had an excellent meal. We spent another day there and then left. It was not a very pretty harbour, with a great deal of diesel and rubbish floating around, and we were glad to leave.

We left to do battle with the Portuguese fishing gear. It was all over the place. That night we had to stop sailing as there was just too much gear. We heaved too, and then out of the gloom came a bamboo with a flag on it, I just had time to grab it and run down the side of the boat with it, and it went clear. Fortunately dawn was not long in coming, we started sailing again and a good sail it was too. Sun and wind for a change. In the afternoon we closed with the port of Penchie. The pilot book showed a small marina, but it was under repair and there was not any space for us. There was however a yellow buoy that I think marked the mooring area although not enough space to anchor, so I lassoed the buoy, pulled it close and dropped a length of chain through its shackle to moor us securely to it. I was sure someone would throw us off. But no, we were left alone that night.

In the morning the local policeman came alongside in an RIB and we filled out a form – the Portuguese are big on forms. He was surprisingly friendly and told us there was space to go in and get fuel. We dropped the mooring, but the chain I put through the bottom shackle had got stuck, so I had to go swimming to sort it. I only needed my snorkel mask and fins, I had a full set of scuba gear aboard, but this time it was not needed. We went in and re-fuelled, and then after tying up to the harbour wall we went off to explore and shop. We were taken by the beauty of the castle, after looking it over we carried on walking to find the internet café. It was shut, but we had a good lunch just across the road in a small cafe. We arrived back just before we went aground on the falling tide, at 16.15 hrs.

On the 19th 10 2010 we left mainland Europe. That was the end of our coast hopping. The next leg would take us into the wide Atlantic Ocean and hopefully the Canaries. But I did say if we were making slow progress we would put into Madeira.

Safely moored up

Chapter 11

The first day was fine, and Helen got some photos of Pilot whales. The night was a stunner; totally clear with lots of stars and frequent meteors. The next day I caught a small Dorado. Helen is not fond of fish, and hates me killing things, so she was less than thrilled. However I soon had it filleted and frying, she did eat a little to keep me happy. The wind was very sporadic and later we had to run the engine to maintain progress. I happened to be watching the oil pressure gauge when the needle dropped from its usual 22 psi to 15.

I stopped the engine. I explained to Helen that there was a problem, and maybe changing the oil and filter would solve it. It's a gruesomely dirty job oil changing on that BMC, it's not an easy spin on filter, you have undo a bolt you can't see, try not to spill anything into the bilges, then renew the filter and replace. Oh and if you get it on wrong, the moment the engine starts it blows all the new oil straight into the bilges, and I only had enough for one oil change! No pressure then. I re-started the engine, the oil stayed in the sump, but the pressure was still lower than usual.

We would have to just sail, the problem was there was no wind, and we slopped around all night. Then the next morning the wind arrived, and we started making progress. Several birds on migration landed on Gloria for a rest, some of them were cute little yellow birds, and I had no idea of what they were. I caught a bigger Dorado, it chased Helen down below. By the time I had killed it the cockpit was running with blood. Helen was less than impressed but what a tasty fish!!

The wind increased and our course became a broad reach. Our new problem was trying to get Gloria to steer herself. I tried about every mix of sails. If there was any mainsail in that mix, Gloria would just round up. She simply would not run with twin head sails. In the end the only way was broad reaching with the jib, staysail, and main staysail and with that rig the autopilot would hold Gloria on course. Just. But that did mean our batteries took a hammering, so I had to run the little genny to keep the batteries topped up.

Because we had taken so long already I decided that we would make for Porto Santos. This was because I knew that Helen's family would be getting worried. We fell into a watch system that left Helen on watch when I expected Porto Santos to come into sight. It was hard for me to stay below, but I wanted Helen to be the first to spot the island. In due course I heard her shout, "Land ho" and I was glad to see the excitement in her face. The island was a harsh piece of volcanic rock in the ocean, which rose high above us as we rounded the headland to reach the marina. I started the engine so we could motor the last half mile. The wind was funnelling around the hills and was quite fresh, and I realised it would be challenging to get moored up without colliding with any other boats.

The wind would be blowing us into a smart French yacht, so we had to get alongside and ropes on cleats fast. I had to turn to port, run before the wind, turn hard to starboard; punch up into the wind, and then another turn hard to port should slew us into the berth, with our sideways skid helping to keep us away from the French yacht. It all went to plan, and we moored up without incident. Thanks partly to a small group of other yachties who stood by to catch our lines. But the French skipper was less than impressed. Then I saw why; one of the gas bottles had been swept over the side, and was dangling by its chain, just like a fender, I think the Frenchman thought we had a strange sense of humour! We arrived on the 26th of October, and had covered the 540 miles in 6.5 days.

One of the people who helped us get safely berthed was Martin, who is German and was sailing with his wife Fraula and new baby Pahla, on a really expensive Malö yacht – about 40' LOA. I had got so used to being snubbed by the posh yachties that I was surprised when he came over to talk to us, we had coffee on Gloria, then more coffee on his yacht. Martin was a keen runner, and I agreed to go with him in the morning. He was a better runner, but slowed down enough so I could keep up.

Porto Santos is amazing to run around, it's big enough to be a challenge but not too big. There are several big hills, and tremendous scenery to struggle around. Helen was in her element, there is a six mile beach at the end of the marina, and the sun was bright and hot. The shops were about two miles down the road, so that was a good walk. At night if we ate out we strolled back home on the beach, listening to the lizards call. The only bad side was the showers at the marina were not very salubrious, and the men's had a resident giant cockroach!

I had another go at the engine, I bought some more engine oil, I could only get 15/40 W and it was massively expensive. Back at the boat I located the drain plug on the sump, previously I had just pumped the old oil out, and I was hoping that my problem might be that there was sludge in the sump. So instead of sucking the old oil out with a special pump I carried, I undid the drain plug, the black mess missed the carefully placed container I had left for it. I refilled the engine with a mixture of oil and diesel to flush the sump. I then ran the engine on tick over for a while, and then emptied it again. I then refilled the engine with clean oil, and put my last oil filter in. As soon as the engine started, the filter blew off, and oil sprayed everywhere. I went and purchased another two gallons of oil. This time I carefully made sure that the oil filter was seated properly before I started the engine again. The oil stayed in the engine, and thankfully the oil pressure was a lot better.

Then the real work could begin. I washed the cabin sole and degreased all the planks, and then I started ladling the black old oil from the deep bilges into old diesel containers. By the time I had the bilges clean I had 15 gallons of oil/bilge water to carry up to the recycling area. The engine sounded a whole lot better; Martin came aboard for a listen and said it sounded like it would run forever, so I went for a clean-up. After a long shower, lots and lots of soap and scrubbing, I was clean as well. A job well done!

We stayed at Porto Santos for 10 days, and enjoyed every moment. We made friends with several other yachties, as well as Martin and his wife. It's a wonderful place; not too built up, but it's the long white beach that makes it outstanding. Far too soon it was time for Helen to fly home, and I went with her to the airport. I had to leave before she left or she would have seen my tears. I could not understand why I felt so emotional, but I did. Back at the boat I went over the weather forecast with Martin. There was a window in a couple of days that would give me fair winds for three days that should get me and Gloria to Grand Canaria. I left two days later, and Martin helped me get out of the berth.

Chapter 12

The first day the wind was hard on the port bow. I could just clear Madeira and the nearby islands. Gloria sailed herself with no input from me all the first day, and the second was the same. During the second night I sighted the flashing light that marks Illhas Selvagens, a group of islands and reefs that have been wrecking boats for thousands of years, I watched carefully as we slipped by them, I would like to visit one day, but you have to have a permit to land there. On the third day the shifted to the north, and I had to steer again.

Gradually the wind died during the next five hours. We got down to two knots, and we spent a whole day crawling along. Slowly Grand Canaria appeared and when we were 10 miles off as darkness came I started the engine, and watched the oil pressure gauge like a hawk. At first it was fine, then after about 10 minutes it started to drop, before long it was down to 7 psi - far too low - but as the engine was sounding fine I let it run at low revs so we could get into the port of Las Palmas. Finally we reached the anchorage and I managed to find space for Gloria amongst the many anchored yachts, we were a long way out from the shore but it was the best place I could find, so I dropped the hook.

The time by then was 22.10 hrs. And the date was 7th November, so the trip had taken 3.5 days, to cover the three hundred and twenty miles. And that was a little bit better than we had averaged before.

The next morning I went in to get a new gauge, after consulting my father about the oil pressure problem he gave a list of things to check, starting with a new gauge, as that might be the problem. I went ashore, or I tried to. The outboard Edmund had lent me had no cooling water coming out the hole. I rang Edmund and asked him if it was like that before, apparently it was. I told him about the oil pressure problem and asked him to bring out a new oil filter.

Then I rowed into the marina at Las Palma. It was a long row, and difficult in the inflatable. I queued up in the Volvo dealership and tried to get a new oil pressure gauge from them, no go. So I went to the chandlery further down the road, there I had to take a ticket to get in the queue! Eventually I was served and to my surprise was told to come back the next day and they would have one. The ARC yachts had filled the marina, and all the local shops were doing a roaring trade. Edmund texted me and gave me the name of a mate of his who was also an engineer who had a yacht in the marina and was part of the ARC. I went and found him, but he was far too busy sorting out his own yacht to come out to Gloria to see if he could suggest anything.

Back at Gloria I went looking for the next item on my father's list which was the oil pressure release. I started exploring the engine and found the valve in the oil filter housing. When I got it out I realised I needed small circlip pliers to fully dissemble it. Another long row ensured. Once ashore I went to the hardware shop and bought the pliers, my hands were sore by the time I reboarded Gloria. I pulled out the vital, irreplaceable circlip, as it emerged from its hole; it pinged off, bounced around a bit and landed by my foot. How the yawning bilge didn't get it I will never know. Once disassembled, I cleaned the valve and stretched the spring out a bit. Then I put it all back again and started the engine. It made a difference, the oil pressure was better, and seemed to stay up to

15psi even when the engine was up to working temperature. Just in case we had any more trouble with it I bought a 50 watt solar panel, and fitted it to the top of the coach roof to trickle charge the batteries.

I managed to clear the outboards waterways and life was looking a bit rosier. Edmund had given me a big light genoa. It was far too big to fit the fore triangle but it fitted the main mast beautifully. However, when I tried to use it, it back winded the main sail. I decided to cut it down and make it fit the fore mast. If I did it by hand I would save a bit of money. It took 3 days to complete, but I was very happy with the result. I had to take it ashore for the sail maker to put the clew ring in. And thankfully they did not laugh at my workmanship. Back at the boat, it fitted very well. A few days later Edmund arrived, and he had brought another crew member with him, a young man called Jack. After a few beers in the very packed sailors bar we went out to Gloria.

We assigned berths. Edmund had used the bench behind the table on the short trip from Battlesbridge to Gosport, and with the excess of the sail I had cut down I made him a lee cloth. I was under the impression that the sail had been a favourite of his, but it turned out he had put it in his loft because the crew had complained that it was a really bad shape, in fact they had nick named it "vinegar tits".

The next day we planned our victualing. Edmund said if we had to hand steer all the way across the Atlantic then another crew member would be a good idea, and there were plenty of people looking for a trip across the Atlantic. Edmund said we should choose one carefully, and interview them to make sure they were competent and would fit in. Later we went to the sailors bar. I went to the toilet but there was a queue. While I was waiting the guy behind me started talking to me and said he was looking for a sail across to the Caribbean. He asked if I had a boat, which I confirmed and said that we were looking for another crew. He seemed okay, so I told him, "If you are on the dock at the dinghy park tomorrow morning at 09.30 I will meet you and take you out to the boat and you can see if you want to sail with us".

Then I took him over to meet the other guys, Edmund said "can I have a word Max?" We walked out; "So what happened to us carefully interviewing candidates?" He went on to point out that picking up blokes out of the toilet in a bar was not what he envisioned as a careful interview procedure. If there had been facilities I think he would have made a cup of tea! "He will be ok" I told him and we left it at that.

The next morning our new man was there at 09.30. Having passed the first test of punctuality I took him out to Gloria. He did not flinch and I was sure we would all get on OK. His name was also Jack, and he was from Belgium, his occupation was computer animation, and he was attempting to get around the world without flying. We got some jobs done, and then went ashore for the evening, we decided we just had to get the food sorted then refuel and top the water tanks up and we could go. Two days would sort it.

The next day was spent victualing, it took several trips with the dinghy to get all the food aboard and I was wondering where the hell it was going to go. I told the two Jacks to stow it in the fore cabin, no-one would be sleeping up there so it could be our main food stowage. But we needed a list of what was where. I went off to get a new dinghy pump as the old one was dead, and some thicker engine oil. I had a long walk before I found a place that sold anything other than 15/40. I managed to get some 20/50 and started the long walk back to the marina, I stepped on some glass, a piece of which went through my flip flop and cut my foot. By the time I arrived back with the new pump the food fetching and stowing had ground to a halt because the old pump had dropped to bits and the dingy was deflated.

I pumped up the dinghy and rounded up the crew from the bar so we could recommence the victualing. Finally it was all bought and put away. The two Jacks had done a good job working out how much food we needed and stowing it with a list of what was were. We sorted out a bunk for the new Jack. The next day I started the engine so we could go in and get fuel, as soon as I opened the sea cock it started to leak, quite a lot. Edmund said "Should it be doing that?" I said "No, I will tighten it up." I put a spanner on the nut, gave it a little tug, and the whole weed trap broke off in my hand! The seacock was still good, but some loony had only put the fitting into it with 1 thread! The thread was blocked and no way would anything screw in, the seacock was in a difficult place to get at, and I could see a boatyard job looming. We did not have the time or the money to prat about, so with an inspired bit of bodging I rammed a plastic pipe in the hole and then was able to jamb the cooling water pipe into that.

We motored into the marina and waited for the fuel pontoon to empty, it was a long wait. A space finally became free and we charged in. Once there we fuelled up and topped up the water tanks. Then we were ready to go, the fuel man wanted us to go out astern , I knew we would have problems like that, and we used a stern spring to kick the bow out then when ahead, "Hasta la vista baby" I shouted to the fuel man, he laughed and we were off!

Replenishing supplies

Chapter 13

My happiness did not last; the wind was fitful and we had to motor sail, but 30 minutes down into the trip the oil pressure dived right down to 5psi. I stopped the engine. The crew rightfully were not happy. After 24 hours of slow sailing, Jack number 1 came to see me and told me he wanted to get off. I was more than a little miffed. Las Palmas was overflowing with people who wanted a trip across the Atlantic, so if he had been harbouring doubts he should have spoken up sooner. His reason for wanting to leave seemed to be that Gloria was not safe. I pointed out that with the EPIRBS Edmund had brought we now had 4 on board. He had also brought a satellite phone, we had a life raft, the inflatable lashed to the coach roof and loads of flares. Edmund had approximately 70,000 miles of ocean sailing under his belt and I had been knocking around boats for almost 40 years, so although Gloria was not bright and shiny, I thought she was safer than most yachts crossing the Atlantic then.

My arguments did not sway him so I told him I was sorry but without an engine we could not go back, we would put into the Cape Verdes, and he could get off there. Two days later, the ARC yachts left, and 48 hours later they started coming past us, the trade wind had not kicked in and we were very slow. Edmund used the satellite phone and we were in daily contact with my dad, and so had weather forecasts. But what we really needed was wind, and there was not a lot of that. Edmund got my sextant out and he started teaching us celestial navigation. We had plenty of time and the watch system we were using gave each of us a whole day off in every four. Well, not really off, because we had to cook and make the tea, but no steering, and no watch keeping. This system was known as the "mother watch system" (see Appendix 2) so we were taking it in turns to be mother, and we soon found out who could cook and who could not!

After a week we had a real no wind calm, the water was so inviting I had to go for a swim, I put a mask and fins on and dropped into a blue world. The temperature was just right and the other lads were soon splashing about as well. I dived under the keel, it was the first time I had seen the whole keel, and the previous time at Hardway when I had her dried out she was sitting on it. I was a bit concerned to notice that there was a fault in the concrete about midway along the bottom of the keel, I put my hand in and a cloud of dirt came out. Because we had no leak and the fault did not seem to go very deeply into the keel I decided that there was nothing I could do and I would not tell the other lads. Soon the wind came back and we started sailing again.

We started catching fish, Dorados, which were very tasty but the fishing gear I had was not strong enough for the bigger fish and I began losing fish and lures at an alarming rate. Morale was quite high, we drew lots for cleaning stations; I got the galley, Edmund the cockpit, Jack number 1 drew the saloon, and Jack 2 got the heads. We also started doing drills, the man overboard threw up a problem - I asked Jack 1 for a winch handle, of course both Jacks went for it, there was a dull thud as two heads clashed, and I realised that one of them would have to change his name. Jack 1 was called John on his passport but he hated that name and insisted on being called Jack, at that point Jack 2 announced with a very un-Belgium like no-nonsense authority that from then on wards he was to be known as "Captain Blood", we were happy to oblige.

One evening the wind disappeared completely, the swell went down, and that night the moon was huge, it was so bright you could have read a book on deck. All around us swam dorados, fish that had turned absolutely golden in colour - it was awesomely beautiful, and hard to believe we were in the mighty Atlantic Ocean. A light wind filled in from the north east and we got underway eventually.

A text message came in on the satellite phone that there was an abandoned catamaran floating about only 120 miles from us so we started sailing towards it. But the wind died again. I had managed to get some thicker oil, so Jack and I did an oil change. The thicker oil brought the oil pressure up a bit and we could use the engine again at low revs. Motoring at 4 knots we went past a deck chair floating about, as we got closer we saw a shark's fin circling it, the fin suddenly vanished, we were towing a fishing lure, the next second the fishing rod bent double and then the line broke.

The shark had struck! I was glad we did not have to get it aboard; it looked very hungry and pissed off. That evening we arrived at the last known position of the cat. Because it was coming down dark we heaved too, then in the morning sailed down what we hoped was the cats track. I was pulled up the foremast by Jack, and that's where I stayed the rest of the day. We did not see the cat, and it brought home to us just how big the ocean is.

We went back on track for the Cape Verdes, and a few days later we saw St Vincent in the distance. A pod of sperm whales was there to welcome us to the land fall. We soon were safely berthed in the marina at Mindello. By then the days had slipped away and it was already the 4th of December. It had taken us 14 days to cover the 900 or so miles. We went ashore for a well-earned beer. Our first problem was no local currency. We went to a cash machine, and none of our cards worked. Back at the marina we had a re think. There were a lot of kids hanging around begging, I asked one of them if he knew of a working cash machine, he led me round the back streets, to a machine that actually worked.

I gave him a tip and went back to tell the other lads. The local bar was a wild place; the beer was good and cheap. So some of us drank too much, Edmund was only drinking on feast days and holidays and so did not over indulge. In the morning I went for a run. Once past the high street the poverty of the place became apparent. The buildings were mostly unadorned grey breeze block and gangs of scruffy dogs roamed the street. The Cape Verdes are part of Africa and have the same problems. I met Edmund on the way back. He had been up for hours and he had been for a long walk during which he had found a man who purported to be a marine engineer, and had made an appointment for him to come on board to see if he could fix the engine.

But first we had to get signed in. Edmund and I went to sort the paperwork out at the immigration and customs office that was inside the docks. Mobs of locals waited in the hot sun, hoping to get some casual work unloading the ships, every now and then a gang was formed from the waiting throng. Once we had the correct bits of paper and stamps in our passports we returned to Gloria to wait for Edmund's engineer. He did show up, but could not make any constructive comments. The only thing I could think of was to put 40w oil in, to get the pressure up that way.

I asked him if he knew where I could get some oil but he did not know. In the end I found the shop that sold oil and I bought a couple of gallons. Another oil change got the pressure up a bit. The other alternative was to go to the local boat yard. But I found out that we would not be able to work on the boat there ourselves and would have to find accommodation ashore. It could take a long time to fix our problem, Edmund very kindly offered to lend me £1500 towards the cost, but I declined. I could not see any way of paying him back, and I did not want to risk our friendship for the sake of money.

Jack number 1 sorted out his plane trip and disappeared. Although he would be missed, we had a lot more space with his absence. We did some more food shopping and bought some eggs and more flour. Each time we left the marina we would be mobbed by kids trying to make a buck. I know they are desperate, but the constant begging became tiresome, and for them to its unhealthy. I don't know what the answer is, but I know giving them money does not work.

One of the locals who went by the name of "Julius Caesar" offered to show us were we could buy fishing gear. He took us to one shop and I bought some big hooks, but they did not have the wire trace I needed. Julius took us to another place, which looked suspiciously like a brothel to me, but in the back was a fishing tackle shop. But the prices were very high. And each time we bought something Julius was getting a commission. After that shop Julius would not leave us alone and his constant yammering and attempting to get us to buy things was getting very annoying, in the end I lost it with him after he kept on asking for money for being our guide. I gave him a couple of euros and told him he was not worth it, as he did not get us any deals and was obviously getting paid at both ends. He was not happy, but did leave in the end.

We had to get some more diesel, big problem; ARC boats were coming in and fuelling up. And super yachts were also doing the same. The lack of trade winds was proving very profitable for the fuel sellers. We got in the queue. There was only one pump. A super yacht spent 4 hours fuelling. He went, and then the next one came in. This one sent a man up the mast and refused to move while he was there, with another few hours being wasted. I tried standing by the pump with our spare fuel cans, but they staff would not fill them up, in between the big yachts.

Despite the queuing yachts, the staff still closed for 2 hours at lunch, and knocked off promptly at 18.00. In the end I got so fed up I walked with Blood to the local garage and filled our cans there. It was a lot more expensive, but we got the 30 gallons we needed. One more chore was to get some more cooking gas, so I took our empty Calor cylinder to the filling place and met a very helpful gentleman who spoke perfect English, as well as many other languages. I felt very ignorant in his presence. He told me to return in an hour and my cylinder would be filled. And it was, result!

Edmund also made a killing - he saw an advert for free anchor chain. Some other yacht was getting rid of 100 foot of chain. He gave the man a bottle of my wine for it, deposited it in the fore cabin and asked me deliver it to the Solent for him! Once more we were ready for the Ocean, or as ready as we could be, but I was worried to hell about the engine, and there was no easy fix. We could use it at low revs for a short time, but to use it longer risked damaging it beyond repair.

Chapter 14

We left the next day, a wonderful breeze soon dropped the islands below the horizon, I caught a small dorado in the dusk, and as I cooked it up we caught another. The wind grew brisker and soon we were doing 7 knots! Whoopee, at last we were really on the way, but of course it did not last and a couple of days later we were back to a wallowing 2-3 knots. But wonderful star filled nights and warm days made up for it somewhat.

The fish we were catching got bigger and bigger, lots of dorado had adopted Gloria as their stalking horse, as she crashed through the waves she often put up flying fish, and the hungry dorados swimming either side of the bow would pounce and gain a meal. Flying fish would often be found on the deck in the morning, we tried to eat them but I found them oily and not very tasty, one morning instead of just throwing the stranded fish back I threaded a wire trace and a large double hook though one, attached it to the line and dropped it in the sea, a tuna hit it before it had time to make a splash, and a tasty lunch was soon flapping on deck.

But that success was followed by an intensely difficult period when the fish got so big none of our gear could hold them. Time after time I would get called up because the reel was zipping out, strike and after a while a big fish would slash its way free of the line. I did manage to land another 12 pound tuna, but it jumped up and drove a hook into poor Edmund who was innocently steering at the time. It was a hilarious if panicky few seconds before Edmond and his new pal were separated, Edmund was first aided by Blood, the tuna was filleted by me.

My celestial navigation lessons were becoming easier, as slowly I began to become more proficient and finding our position. Although we were a man down, we all got just about enough rest in between our watches, we were doing 2 hours on 4 hours off, and taking turns in cooking the three daily meals. Captain Blood had turned into a very useful hand he could steer a course as well as anyone and was always cheerful and enthusiastic. We often played a game of Edmund's invention, which if I remember correctly was called "name a famous Belgium". Matters came to a head when we were discussing Castro, and then of course Che Guevara, "His bodyguards were both Belgium" Captain Blood triumphantly declared, "probably why he died so young" I said. Well Edmund thought it was funny!

And so our days went on, mostly good humoured and heavenly, with the only fly in the ointment being our painfully slow progress. On average was about 70 miles per day which meant we would be spending Christmas at sea and New Year as well! In an effort to get our speed up we held on to sail a bit longer than was wise and the goose neck on the main sail broke, this was a big problem as without the goose neck we could not roller reef and no other way of reefing was possible. I soon had a repair on the boom, but now the main was either full up or down. Other notable breakages were the split pin coming out of the clevis pin on the forestay, (spotted by Ed) and the pivot bar on the cooker being cut through by the gimbals. The heads catch failed. The fisherman sail kept getting torn. Edmund took on the mantel of "sail maker" along with his other duties, and repaired the rips.

During a particularly slow watch on the way to St Lucia I wrote this poem:

Becalmed.

So little wind, we put the sails away.

Only 28 miles made good today.

Far from home and St Lucia.

I pulled the Graveyard watch, it made me stare.

Silver light from a big new moon.

Lit the stage, chasing away the gloom.

Golden fish glided silently by.

A scene so tranquil it made me sigh.

Chapter 15

Before we knew it the 25th was upon us. I was hoping to catch a big dorado for dinner, and on Christmas morning I was called from my sleep by the shout of "fish!" from the cockpit. The reel was screaming, I leaped from my bunk grabbed the rod and striking, drove the hook home. The rod bent double and the fish jumped clear and "tail walked" across the sea before racing past the boat. This performance went on for about 30 minutes, then finally the huge dorado lay quietly behind the boat, I reached down with the boat hook, the fish gave a strong twist, broke the line, and was gone. Christmas dinner was a nut roast and a cake we baked. We drank the small amount of brandy and madeira we had left on board. Edmund taught us the words to a song "Have some madeira my dear", at least I think that's what it was called, and anyway we sang that and a few carols and felt happier!

Of course the next morning I hooked another monster and this time with the help of a gaff that Edmund made we actually landed it. We ate dorado all that day, and all the next, on the third day I could not eat it any more, Captain blood baked a loaf, and for some strange Belgian reason baked a piece of fish in it, some kind of surprise dish I think. Well I was surprised!

Because we did not have a working engine we had to keep our power consumption to a minimum, and apart from the 50 watt solar panel our only other way of making electricity was the small Chinese genny. The Honda generator was not working and refusing to run properly when it did start up. So of course we could not make enough power to run any kind of refrigeration. This gave us a problem when we started catching big fish - there are only so many meals you can eat that are fish, before it starts to get very tedious!

Our other food supplies were holding up very well. When I did breakfast I made porridge, Edmund would do Spanish Omelette, and Blood would serve cereals. For lunch we either had fresh fish or pate on toast. Dinner tended to be more adventurous, and could be anything. I usually cooked pulses, lentils, chick peas, and made veggie curries. The advantage of so much fish coming on board was that we did not have to use so much of our other food.

I was hoping to be in St Lucia for New Year but we had no chance, and as that holiday found us still more than a week away I could sense morale starting to flag. It was time to break out the last alcoholic beverage aboard - a bottle of sparkling pink stuff that no-one had the courage to try before. I popped the cork and we all tried a glass. It was horrid so the fish got the rest, it was that bad! Edmund noted that we were at that point officially an alcohol free vessel, and we looked forward to arriving somewhere.

The goose barnacles were starting to grow on Gloria, and that was beginning to slow us down even more, then the wind in the last week went north east and started to blow like a proper trade wind and we even had the odd squall and torrential rain. At last our slow progress brought us into the range of local fishing dories. They were 40 miles out and hand lining for tuna, once spotted they made for us, I suppose that they know that tuna and Dorados are attracted to boats crossing. I felt a bit sad for our late companions as some of them were caught. But it was a slightly worrying time the fishermen in their outboard driven dories, look a lot like the pictures I had seen of pirates. So if we had weapons on board would we have got them ready when we saw the fishermen approaching? And how would these perfectly harmless men have felt? As it was we got a good welcome and plenty of smiles were exchanged.

That evening at long last St Lucia showed up. The wind was very light and I started the engine to get past the last few miles of Atlantic ocean, I went off watch and tried to get my head down, hardly had said head hit the pillow when I heard "Get Max, the steering's gone", I came up and sure enough with a deep foreboding I found the tiller had no resistance and made no difference to our course. I stopped the engine, and then to huge relief I found that it was just a pin that had sheared. I then bashed a bolt into the hole and the repair allowed us to get going again, Edmund said "12 minutes, Max. You are getting fast at fixing things!"

That was the last barrier to getting into Rodney Bay; it was pitch black but we found a space to anchor in twenty foot of water. We had crossed the Atlantic Ocean!!! With the sails off and engine quiet we could take in the fact of our accomplishment. Certainly we had been slow but we had done it, in a yacht that cost less than a good set of waterproof yachting clothing. We then tried to get some sleep.

Fish!

Chapter 16

In the morning we went swimming as the water was so inviting it would have been a crime not to. At about 09.30 I called the marina and asked if they had any space, which they did so we went in. Rodney Bay marina is stuffed with really posh yachts, and Gloria looked a bit out of place amongst her expensive sisters. But we had to check in, and we had jobs to be done, and anyway I thought that we deserved a bit of luxury. Edmund and I went off to the customs to do the paper work.

As we entered the office an officer shouted at me, "Why you not say good morning!" I thought he was having a joke, and gave him the good morning he wanted, but then the next customs officer gave me a bad tempered dressing down for having the audacity to ask to borrow a pen. Thank goodness all our paper work was in order and we had a clearance certificate from the Cape Verdes. We had left the Canaries without a clearance simply because it was so difficult to get one. When the customs man saw in my form that I had not declared a fire arm he berated me for that too; "what do you think you are doing, sailing about the Caribbean without a gun?" I told him guns scared me which seemed to satisfy him and we were checked it. At the marina office we paid for a few nights. Then we went to the cash machine and got some of the local currency, east Caribbean Dollars, there were roughly 4 dollars to a pound.

I had to get a part made to fix the goose neck, so I stripped off the broken bit and went for a walk towards the boat yard we could see. The sun was beating down by then and I wanted to relax, but Gloria had to be fixed first. At the boat yard I was let in after I woke the sleeping security guard so she could open the gate. Once inside I had to find "the China man". I found his workshop, but it was shut. Leaving there I went to the hardware store and bought some more fishing gear. That took up 30 minutes and then I went back to the boatyard. The China man was in and I told him what I wanted; the fitting that had broken had to be copied but made out of stainless steel. He said he could do it, then we started on the price, in the end he would charge me £130 in sterling and it would be ready tomorrow. The price was a bit high, but acceptable. That job taken care of I went back to Gloria, to find that my ship mates had discovered Mount Gay rum, and were busily experimenting with cocktails. I joined them as the rest of the day turned into night, and almost into day again before we fell asleep.

The next morning was a little embarrassing, Gloria looked like a ship wreck, empty bottles and glasses, plates, half eaten food and my best sunglasses, sat on and broken, filled the cock pit. Breakfast was eaten by a subdued crew. Edmund as per usual was chirpy and most annoyingly had gone for an early morning walk - I don't know where he gets his energy from. We had a clean-up and after lunch I went to see the China man again. True to his word my fitting was ready, and a good piece of work it was too. Very strong and later when Blood and I fitted it, it went straight in. Our next job was to install an opening hatch in the galley. I already had it, but I had never needed to fit it, but with the stifling heat we needed as much ventilation as possible. Blood and I installed it and the hatch made a big difference, letting in a lot more light and air.

I spoke to Helen and confirmed that she would be arriving on the 13th, but she also told me she would be landing at Vieux Fort, the other end of St Lucia, this meant it would be cheaper if we sailed Gloria down to Vieux Fort, because the only other way of getting there was a private taxi and that meant a 100 mile round trip, over some very bad roads, thanks to the hurricane that had hit some months earlier. Captain Blood was going to leave us and go to Martinique. And Edmund had made arrangements to meet some friends in Bequia and join their yacht "Stealaway". A party was called for, and it sort of went on for a couple of days!

Eventually the time came to say "good bye" to Captain Blood and I went with him to Customs to get him off the boat's paper work. But we had to deal with the bad tempered customs guy again, it was going quite well, until he asked me when Gloria was leaving, I said "tomorrow" and he said to Blood, and you are leaving today?" The Blood said "No, I thought I would hang about a bit. "The Customs man shouted "immigration!" and pointed at another desk, we went there and the guy told us that he would not let Blood off our paper work unless he could see a ticket to a flight or a ferry ride off the island. We went off to get a ferry ticket, but of course they work on cash and don't give tickets, and they don't even have a schedule, but just show up at the dock.

Our saviour this time was a local celebrity chef called Fernandez. We had become friendly with him and his wife, and when he heard our problem he said, go up there and say "Blood's staying with me; on our boat until he leaves", so I went to see the pit-bull customs man and told him that, to my utter amazement he smiled and said, "that's all right then" and stamped our papers! I bought one of Fernando's books off him to say thank you, not the "Cooking with Ganja" one but another on Caribbean cooking.

113

The next day we said good bye to Captain Blood and various new friends we had made. Edmund and I motored Gloria out of Rodney Bay and set the sails. We had a cracking good sail down the island, until we turned past the extinct volcano of Sophia, the wind swung around and came from more ahead, it was okay at first and we built up speed, but soon we could not lay out course and started tacking. As darkness fell Edmund told me to watch for a flashing red light that was on a cliff and would mark the rocks near the anchorage we wanted. We soon picked up the red flashing light, but it looked low to me, we closed with it and by then the wind had freshen up to about a force seven, and it was raining, the red light was too close and too low, I put the boat around onto the port tack, just before we hit the super yacht that was using a red flashing light for an anchor light! The red flashing light on the shore was not working. We found a place to anchor and dropped the hook.

Going for a dip in the Caribbean

Chapter 17

After breakfast the next morning I inflated the dinghy and we went into the small harbour. I was hoping we would find a place alongside the wall, but the harbour was very shallow and there was not a lot of space. Tying up by the other dinghies, a tall man sprinted towards us, he was a fisherman and by the look of his build someone you wanted on your side, he said " I look after your boat" , "how much" I asked, " 10 dollar" , by then I had learnt that the proper response to this was "east Caribbean?"   "Yah man" he replied, and the deal was done. Edmund and I went off to explore. Talk about culture shock! Vieux Fort is off the tourist routes, and is a bit like the Mexican towns I used to see in films such as "Butch Cassidy and the Sundance Kid", and it definitely had an edgy feel to it. We stopped at a bar/shack to refresh ourselves. While we sipped our carib beers a local came in drank some rum, and after protracted negotiations, he had it put on his slate, and at least I think that's what was going on!

We wondered off to find the airport. It was a bit of a walk but not that far, and every time a local taxi van saw us walking they would stop and try and get us to get in. Nice of them, but we really wanted to walk. Once at the airport we had a spot of lunch. I had already spotted that a good policy was never ever to eat beef burgers when dining out, and this policy had allowed me to avoid the bad tummies that the rest of the lads had suffered in the Cape Verdes. Unfortunately Edmund had not learnt this yet; he had the beef burger and chips I had the goat curry. We waited for Helen to land, and then she was there - it was so good to see her.

Helen wanted to go to a hotel for the first night to acclimatise, so we found a nice one that overlooked the anchorage. It was quite cheap and very pleasant. Edmund had dinner with us. Helen had brought out Christmas presents for me from her and my family. She had also brought me a new set of glasses to replace the ones I had lost during the recent party, and it was very good to be able to see properly again. Amongst the pressies from her was a Sony digital book; at last I was not going to run out of stuff to read as it had about 100 books loaded on it.

But possibly the most precious thing she brought out apart from herself was a huge bag of Tetley teabags!! Ed went back to Gloria, Helen and I stayed. It was the first bed I had slept in for approximately four months. In the morning Edmund arrived back from the boat and had breakfast with us. He explained that he had not had a lot of sleep on account of the mild food poisoning he had endured all night. We were glad we missed the performance - boats are too small for that kind of thing! We took Helen aboard and sun bathed most of the rest of the day, very relaxing.

Helen and I were taken by Edmund ashore the next morning, our mission was to get clearance to depart, and fortunately there was a customs office in Vieux Fort according to the pilot book. Edmund and I had seen it on the way to the airport, so that's where I took Helen. It was the wrong office, and we found out that we had to go to the docks. It was quite a long walk in the heat, but we got there OK, only to have the gates slammed in our faces by a security guard. I tried to go through a gap and she went ballistic!

After shouting at a lorry driver for a bit, she let us in - well weird! We then went to the customs office. There was a big queue and we patiently waited for our turn. The customs man was berated by a good looking lady also queuing, she told him to speed it up, he smiled, and he did speed up. We got our clearance papers and stamps with no problem, and he was very friendly. We also managed to contact Edmund on Gloria and he was able to pick us up from the docks rather than us walk to the fishing harbour. We were going to leave that night, bound for Bequia. I took the dinghy ashore for a bit of final food shopping and I bought four cold beers on the way back. The scary looking man who was taking care of the dinghy insisted I view his mate's tourist trinkets.   I was so impressed by the artistic quality of the pendants he had made that I bought one for Helen, and I gave a cold beer to the minder, to my surprise he hugged me, and said" there is no difference between us". Once more I felt like I had missed something important, but I could not help being moved by these people. They had so little material possessions and money, but they smiled a lot and seemed to live very full lives. That night we left.

The wind was near gale force once off the coast, huge seas battered us, poor Helen was sick, and I had to make up a bed for her by the engine to keep her from getting flung about. The truly evil bit was over once we reached the lee of St Vincent, but then we had too little wind and it took ages to get past. With the coming of daylight we got clear of Saint Vincent, but the wind shifted and headed us and blew hard again. By now we were all fed up, and against my better judgement I started the engine so we could motor sail and get into Bequia faster. After a couple of hours the oil pressure suddenly dropped to nothing. I stopped it straight away. And we had to tack into the anchorage without it.

I changed the headsail for the working one and was very glad I did so, because suddenly a squall hit us. The wind went up to about a force 9 and the rain came down so hard I could not breathe without putting a hand over my mouth to deflect the water. Edmund had the helm and called the depth, and at 20 foot I asked him to bring us into the wind. I wanted to drop the anchor while we were moving so we could dig it in a bit as I was aware that the pilot book said the holding was poor. I dropped the anchor a tad too soon, and Gloria span on the chain when I snubbed it, it was not a pretty arrival, but we did not hit any other boats and we did not break anything, so I guess it was successful.

Once stopped Helen and I set the other anchor at an angle to the Bower anchor. Then Edmund and I put on snorkel and masks and checked the gear. The bower had dragged so I dug it in a bit and put a rock on it, the other anchor was set, but not very well.

Chapter 18

Edmund and I went ashore to check in. As I locked up the dinghy and out board, an American said "What you think anyone going to steal that piece of shit." I resisted the temptation to slap him and Edmund ignored him - pointedly - he was good at that! In the customs office I had forgotten a pen again, so before it all kicked off I went and bought one from the shop next door. Our checking in was painless after that, not so the French crew who had elected to turn up in swim suits, they were being ignored by the officials when we came in, and were still being ignored when we left!

We went for a well-earned beer in a nearby bar. After this refreshment we moved on to the vegetable market. I wanted some tomatoes, and the next minute I was surrounded by Rastas all shouting and demanding I bought other products. There was some stuff I wanted but it all got out of hand, I spent all the money I had in the end, about twenty pounds, and I had a big bag of fruit and veg, but it was not a pleasant shopping experience and we avoided the place for the rest of our stay.

We went back to Gloria, on the way we saw Edmund's friends, so after we picked up Helen and her beach kit, Edmund dropped us on a handy pier near the beach and went off to Stealaway. Helen was like a pig in pooh at first, miles and miles of empty beach, but after a short while she gave a squeak and said there was a crab looking at her, out of a hole, which there was. What was more the whole beach had crab holes and we were even sitting on some! Helen demanded we adjourn to the nearby bar pronto. Later that day we had dinner on Stealaway and made friends with Martin and Helen.

Edmund left Gloria the next day after my Helen had given us both a short haircut, moving into Stealaway. They were going to Union Island the later, Edmund only had another week and he would have to go home, so he wanted to see as much as possible. Gloria was strangely quite without him. I don't think you can sail the miles we had and have the adventures we had without bonding. I won't pretend we always saw eye to eye, but I had and always will have huge amounts of respect and admiration for him.

Helen wanted to see more of the island, so we went for walks, and had dinner in some of the restaurants. I was able to get the gas bottle Chris Lewis had lent me filled up. The sail maker replaced all the hanks on the number 1 jib at quite a reasonable charge. I even found a shop that sold paraffin. I wanted to use a hurricane lamp for the anchor light, but it kept going out in the frequent squalls. Lots of yachts anchored in the bay, but there were not many places were the holding could be relied upon We got away with it because our bower anchor is twice the size recommended for a 38 foot yacht, to that we had 150 foot of 10mm chain, and then another anchor a 45 lb. CQR with 15 foot of 10mm chain and 150 foot of 12mm nylon. The charter yachts that frequently anchored near us did not have such heavy gear and consequently in the heavy squalls they often dragged.

One of the things of big concern to me was the state of our dinghy - it had started to deflate rapidly. Each day I had to inflate it and we were anchored a long way off, so by the time we were in it was getting distinctly wobbly and then we would have to inflate it for the return trip. Helen was getting very nervous about it, as was I. We looked around for another one but the local chandleries had no dinghies for sale. There was one large RIB, but apart from being too big, the man wanted £700 for it. So when we called in to the offices of Caribbean Compass, to see Sally and Tom, who are old friends of my father and my stepmother. We asked them if they knew of any dinghies for sail. They didn't but wanted to know all about our adventures and how my father and step mother were doing. My father used to write articles for them.

I started to think we would have to make a hard dinghy; the problem was where to do it. We could not make it on the beach at Bequia as there was not any secure space. Looking around I did find one bashed up scruffy boat that would have done us for a while, but after a couple of days of asking about I discovered that the owner was still using it and did not want to sell it. We decided to move on. That night I was sitting in the cockpit mulling over our dinghy problem when I noticed a darker shadow amongst the blackness, I shone our steamer scarer and in the light saw an inflatable with an outboard drifting by! It would have vanished by the time I had inflated ours, so after shouting for Helen to come up I slipped over the side, swimming to it I was able to tow it back to Gloria where I made it fast.

That was the easy bit. What to do next, a moral struggle ensued, and in the end I grabbed the radio mike and on channel 16 I asked if anyone had lost a dinghy. A local boat man answered and asked our location, I told him and about an hour later he showed up and said I should give him the dinghy, I told him that I would hang onto it; the owner would surely come looking for it in the morning. He was cross, but he left, and I put a steel cable and a padlock on the dinghy. At first light there came a knocking on our hull, a much relieved man called Bruce Burman, from the yacht "Plane Song", came to collect his property, he came back shortly with a bottle of wine and 100 EC dollars as a thank you. He was a very pleasant man and I was glad we had taken the honourable route.

Chapter 19

We left Bequia a day or so later, and we had a great sail down to Canouan. We anchored by a green beacon in 22 foot of water and I went down with the snorkel and checked the hook was dug in. It was, so I slept well that night. The next morning we decided against going ashore, as the view was uninspiring, so we sailed onto Mayreau. I had seen the photos in the pilot book; Saltwhistle Bay looked truly beautiful, and it was, but it was also very crowded so we picked a spot, tacked up to it brought her into the wind, dropped the anchor and prayed, fortunately it held. I got another one out; a small fisherman that I dived on to make sure it was well dug in. Then we could relax. Almost. Our activities had drawn us to the attention of a local, who came aboard and asked us what the problem with the engine was. I told him, he said" We can fix that" I asked him how much "£700" , I asked him how he would get it out, he said it would be no problem and that me and Helen could come and stay with him while he fixed it. I asked him where he would get the parts from, to which he replied that he could get them from St Vincent. For a while he had me going but the more he talked the more I realised that if we put ourselves in his hands we would probably never sail out again. I told him we would think about his offer.

We went back to relaxing. A French catamaran came in, it had three very beautiful girls sunbathing topless on the foredeck, Helen said, "he's going to hit us" and she was right, I called out and said "You won't hurt us, but you will damage your boat." The topless beauties did not move a finger; I put a fender down and helped the skipper push off. It was all very surreal! Later we went ashore and climbed the very steep hill to the village. There was a bar dedicated to Bob Marley, the owner was teaching the very beautiful girls from the catamaran to sing Bob Marley songs, Ganja smoke filled the air and the French skipper looked on in a trance of pure rapture.

Outside it had started to rain hard and we took shelter in a café. There some locals were playing dominoes with such passion I think it could safely be described as extreme dominoes. We sipped our coffee and stayed out of the way. The rain stopped, we went to the local shop, bought a few bits, then went up to the church. The view was superb; we could see the whole of Tobago Keys from there. It was beautiful, but no place for an engineless concrete schooner that's shorthanded, because it had a great many yachts already there. We reluctantly decided to give it a miss.

We made friends with a couple of Brits on a yacht called "Wind Dragon". The owner had a compressor on board. He was teaching his girlfriend scuba diving and they asked me if I would like to join them on her first dive. It was a nice dive. We came back with some old conch shells and Helen was very pleased with that. And as an added bonus, Shane refilled my dive cylinder afterwards. We loved the bay, it is classic Caribbean, white sands, palm trees, and blue seas, but it gets very crowded we decided to move on. This became a problem, because there were so many boats around, we needed control, so we had to be moving and I made a big mistake by setting too much sail once we had retrieved the main anchor, the sails filled and Gloria broke the other anchor out - literally; it ripped the flukes right off it! It was the small fisherman and because it was collapsible it had a weak point at the end of the shaft. It was a sad loss because I had owned it for many years.

Our next island was to be Union as the main anchorage was too crowded for us, but only a couple of miles away were another anchorage by Frigate Island. Apart from the disadvantage of a longish dinghy ride it looked like a good place to be. We had the usual wonderful sail, and then we started tacking up for the anchorage as I wanted to get as close to the shelter as possible and we had to weave carefully in and out of the yachts already lying there. Including the avoidance of a 60 foot ketch, all the tacks came off clean and Helen put her into the wind to get the way off her so I could let the anchor go in 15 foot of water, we came to rest between an American Yacht and a big catamaran. We were well away from either vessel. I let out 60 foot of chain at first meaning to let another 40 or so foot out later. I was hailed by the skipper of the American yacht, "you are too close" and his wife chimed in "an howaya gonna get out of here" I waved back gave it another 70 foot of chain and we slipped back.

A small Folkboat called Freya was also anchored there. Her skipper came over and we chatted, and we invited him and his beautiful young wife over for a beer. They came bringing the highest of luxuries - cold beer!!! We got along famously - they were from Germany and had sailed that tiny boat all the way from Portugal. He was called Max and she was called Goorda. Helen was amazed that they had no toilet, just a bucket each! After a couple of hours of this, a RIB came past with the owners of the large posh yacht, we invited the aboard. They were called Christine and Duffy- they ran their yacht as a charter operation. A good party developed. We had such a good time and we were sad to see them all go.

The next morning we went ashore. There were a couple of small boat yards so we went into one of them, meeting man called

Regan. I said "I need a new dinghy mine is going down," He showed me a couple of boats he had made out of the bases of old ribs, but they were far too heavy. We talked about him making me one from plywood. We eventually agreed on £250 and one week. That evening Chris and Duffy called us over for drinks, the crew of Freya was also there and some Canadians from another yacht. We had a great time. And both I and Helen fell in love with Chris and Duffy's yacht. They had a successful charter operation. A lot of their clients had been coming year after year and now they even carried a de-fibulator in case of heart attacks. Christine's father had owned the pilot cutter "Madcap" and she was brought up sailing that fine old lady, Christine and her sister developed a technique for hoisting the mainsail, it involved jumping with the throat halyard and swinging it around the mast to keep the tension.

They were not at all stand offish, and I began to understand why; they were both the real thing. Duffy owned a bit of land on Union and I was talking with him about the dinghy I was going to have made, he said "It's not going to happen, it does not work like that, I could make one in that time, but they won't". Sadly he was right, I checked a couple of times and Regan said it was all under control, but at the end of the week, there was no dinghy, not even a trace of one. So I told him not to bother.

I was able to do a lot of snorkelling around the reefs near Frigate Island, and I went out fishing with Max, he caught a good sized Mutton Snapper, I made it into a fish curry and we had another good night aboard Gloria. Freya was going north and Max asked us to take photos of them sailing about, we were happy to do so. They put their lovely boat in a container on Martinique and had it delivered back to Germany.

One of the many idyllic anchorages

Chapter 20

It was time for us to move on; I had heard good things about a boat yard in Carriacou at a bay called Tyrell. So we went into town to get our clearance papers and stamps. There was a small problem for us to solve before we could go, those lovely Americans had upped anchor at one point, but put a buoy down where their place was, then when they came back they anchored closer to us! It was no problem in the end; I put our other anchor out on the port bow winched up to the bower and when it weighed the port anchor kept us clear of the American yacht.

We sailed off to Hillsborough; the only fly in the ointment was the sail was far too short. We anchored near the pier, and went ashore to check in. The customs and immigration were staffed by friendly people and there were no problems checking in. A local was on the pier looking at our rather saggy dinghy, I asked him if he knew of small dinghies for sale, he said he would ask around.

I and Helen went off to explore, we found a museum, and had a look around, then the tourist guide centre, Helen collected all the leaflets. There was also a really good internet café so we were able to answer all our e mails, and catch up on Facebook. We did some shopping and went back to Gloria. A big Danish schooner had anchored next to us in our absence, and the crew were in the water, splashing around, a stunning blond lovely climbed out then dived back in. I was fascinated, mostly because she was nude, as was the rest of the crew. Helen caught me looking and my punishment was to take off my shorts and dive in as well, it was such a hard life!

We decided to do some more exploring and walked around and out of town, and I was still looking for someone who would build us a dinghy. We stopped and talked to a man who made furniture, his work was exquisite, but he had lots of work on and did not have time to start building boats. We headed back to be beach and met a couple of young guys who were outside one of the small houses, we were talking to them and one of them said that Tyrell Bay was the place to look for a dinghy, then they kind of attached themselves to us and showed us to a bar on the beach, one of them disappeared for a short while, then came back.

We bought them and ourselves bottles of beer. Suddenly Helen looked at Gloria, you could just see her in the anchorage, there was a dory alongside and several guys were holding on, and looked like they were about to board! Helen turned to our new friends, "is that your mates, have you set us up" she asked as I sprinted down the beach, kicking off my flip-flops as I went. I scaled the pier and reached the dinghy park just as the dory I had seen came alongside. The guy at the motor looked up and said "Hi, we found a boat for you." Boy did I feel stupid! The boat he had found was too big and heavy, but I did appreciate the trouble he had gone through. And we saw one of the lads we were with and apologised for any misunderstanding, he just thought we were funny.

Hillsborough is the capital of Carriacou, but the anchorage can get very rolly, so after a few more days we decided to move on to Tyrell Bay. Everything was made ready for sea I hoisted the main sail, main staysail and staysail. I had made a mistake, been lazy and not put the kedge anchor out, with the manual windlass it was a long slow business recovering the bower anchor. By the time I got it up we were sailing and I had a heart stopping moment when I thought our anchor that was only just broken out would catch in another boats anchor chain. Fortunately it didn't and we went clear, gybed round and headed down the coast. We sailed in between a large square rigged ship that was anchored off paradise beach, and past the yachts at the sandy island anchorage. We rounded a headland and saw the Sisters Rocks standing out of the beautiful turquoise sea, and the moored up tugs to our port showed the start of Tyrell Bay, and soon after we were in and tacking through the anchored yachts. We had to get close to the boatyard, but space was getting a bit tight. I saw a patch large enough just up from the first of the moorings, Helen brought Gloria onto the wind, as she slowed up and stopped with flapping sails I dropped our anchor, the one that had never ever dragged, the one I could always depend on, and guess what? You are right; we started dragging, slowly towards an expensive yacht! But salvation was at hand, I put the helm hard over to starboard and we closed with a mooring buoy, it was a piece of cake to pick it up and then recover our anchor that had a rock jamming the flukes! The people watching thought I did it on purpose!

And one of those was Jerry Stewart, a legend, the owner of several tugs and the boat yard. Jerry sailed a small gaff cutter out to Barbados about 30 years before and had stayed, a thoroughly good bloke. A great example being in the year before during the worst drought anyone had known, he towed a barge down to Grenada and had it filled with fresh water and then towed it back so that the locals had water for their livestock.

After we had put the covers on the sails we went ashore. It was Sunday so the boatyard was closed, but the people we met were friendly and I felt at home immediately. We ate ashore at the

Slipway restaurant; this establishment was run by Jerry's Italian wife, a lovely lady called Danni. The restaurant itself used to be the main slipway and still retained the old power saws, nicely made into tables, and the bar was an old planning machine with a hardwood top. It was incredibly cosy, and the food was the best we ever had in the Caribbean, the chef was a lady called Kate, and I was always impressed by the variety and quality of the meals served up.

That's where we first met Jerry; he was drinking a rum punch, there were several of his cronies around and soon we were accepted into this little group. One of the guys there called Tim was from near Battlesbridge and knew the River Crouch really well. He had a black yacht called "Saga" that had an electric engine that hardly ever worked. Quite often we would see him sailing up to his mooring right by the beach. Jerry was the owner and skipper of the yacht "Bloody Mary" a Hughes 38 my father had owned one, and I knew of their sailing qualities.

I went to see Jerry in his boatyard the next day, first of all I asked him if he had any dinghies around I could buy, he told me it was a common problem, and he did not have any, and that he could get me a new one from the chandlery but that would cost about $1800 American! I obviously could not afford to pay that much, but he did agree I could use a patch of ground behind some stored boats so I could build my own. I went and fetched Helen and we went into town to order some wood. I had no plans but a rough idea of what I needed.

At the wood merchants I bought two sheets of exterior 6mm ply and one sheet of 12 mm ply, and six lengths of one by two pitch pine battens, a sheet of polythene and several sheets of sandpaper. The wood yard delivered it and gave me a lift too. It was raining really heavily by the time we reached Tyrell Bay, and I was stunned that the driver would risk his van on the steep muddy drive of the boat yard; it's really a goat track! However, it was all safely landed, and tucked up under the sheeting I bought. Then I went out to Gloria and got my tools together.

I had also a big metal box filled with assorted cross head screws made of hard gold anodised steel, these had been a gift from Del in Galleons Point marina, he said at the time, "these will come in handy for you " how right he was. Once ashore again I started work, I made a framework with the pitch pine battens. That's as far as I got the first day. I went and collected Helen from her new hide out which was the yacht club run by Trevor, the waitresses were Tracy and Chantal, nice friendly girls who kept the place going and always had a smile for their customers. When I went there I met "Hutch" he was using the Wi-Fi to send his e mails, he is a small boat sailor par excellence, and builds these clever sailing canoes that come to bits for stowage on his small yacht. He was interested in my project and was all for rounding up some plans, building moulds and so forth. I told him, maybe the next one I will do that, but I need a dinghy now! We went back to Gloria had dinner and had an early night.

I had an early start on the dinghy, slowed down a bit by having to spend a bit of time blowing up the inflatable - it was almost sinking when I climbed into it. I wedged a big fender under the outboard to stop that from submerging. Once on site I cut out the stern and bow pieces from the thick plywood and screwed them in place. Then I cut out the side pieces. Some of the local shipwrights were working on an old fishing boat and we got chatting, I saw the work they were doing, they had very old worn tools but with the minimum of equipment they could still turn out a top rate job. They were not the least bit patronising about the boat I was making. Another guy, nick named "Slow" sat under a boat most of the day, for the shade, freeing up scaffold clips and greasing them.

By the end of the second day the sides were on, and I was using a kind of sikaflex to stick and waterproof the joints. The third day went fast and we had arguably a boat shape, I say arguably because Helen put pictures on Facebook and Max of Freya (he was back in Germany by then) said that it looked more like a coffin for me! The fourth day started badly. I was up early, but the inflatable dinghy had sunk! The outboard was under water, I got it out and dried it off, then washed off the salt water, and I then saturated it with WD40 and drained the carb. With clean fuel it started up second pull, it was a 4 stroke Mariner, and a very good piece of kit, no water had found its way into the crankcase. So I did not have to change the oil. I inflated the dinghy and rowed it ashore, I found Jerry and told him about the disaster, and he was good enough to lend me a big fiberglass dinghy.

I did not get much of a chance to do any work on the dinghy all that day, Helen and I took the boat Jerry had lent me into the Mangroves to explore. Neither of us have ever been in a mangrove swamp before and we were impressed by the quietness and unspoilt quality of the environment. There was one large Ferro cement yacht that might one day sail, but apart from that there were a couple of old fishing boats and an old tug, all were sunk and gradually being assimilated into the swamp. In the clear water we could see fish and part of the reef, the waterway twisted and turned through the trees. Local bylaws mean that boats cannot anchor in there unless under threat of hurricane. Apparently the mangroves are the place to be if the big winds come in. After being suitably impressed we motored back, and stopped off to pay a visit to Hutch.

Hutch is an American who used to be an aircraft pilot. He got out of the rat race many years ago and had been living a simple life in the Caribbean ever since, he is a writer and is always getting articles printed in the Caribbean paper. He's also working on a book. We drank coffee with him and had a lively conversation, we invited him to have dinner on Gloria some time, but he said he never visited other boats after dark – as to why I never found out. After that we went back on board Gloria and had an early night.

The fifth day working on our new tender ended with something that was definitely a boat, one of the shipwrights asked me how much I wanted for one of my planes, I had two, one old one I had bought really cheaply, that was my favourite, I gave him the other one. Later on the boss of the gang (Leroy) asked me when I was launching, I said "Thursday", "ok we will be there for the blessing" it took me a while to realise he was not taking the piss, but quite serious. The tender was given a covering of epoxy and glass cloth, painted white outside and pastel green inside, and fitted with a rubbing strake of pitch pine. I was able to salvage the rowlocks from the old inflatable and the oars, so we had a boat, all it needed was a name, and it would get that on Thursday! The big day arrived and I was really nervous; what if it did not float? I did some research (asked Jerry) and he told me a West Indian boat blessing involves killing something and splattering blood on the bow! I had a word with Leroy and he allowed that we could use just beer if Helen had big objections to dead chickens and blood, so I went off and got a crate of Carib.

The appointed time arrived and one of the guys helped me slide "Helen" (what else could I call it) into the water, relief, and no leaks! Leroy and the others solemnly dripped beer over her bow and gave her their best wishes, it was a big honour. Then Helen and I rowed around in her for a bit. She was a surprisingly good boat; nice and stable, not too difficult to row and carried Helen, 12 gallons of water, the outboard and me without sinking, success! It's only failing was it was heavier than I wanted. It was a struggle to drag it up the beach. I returned Jerry's boat to him and asked him how much I owed him for renting the patch of ground I had used, "It's ok Max, nothing." I left thinking what a top bloke he was.

She may not be a looker, but she floats!

Chapter 21

One of Gerry's staff was a man called Gus, a big well-made islander who could fix anything. I would quite often see him skippering the small workboat (Dr Pepper) around, always smiling. He had a dog called Rambo - a sort of Labrador; black and a great swimmer. Rambo lived on Gus's yacht which was a big steel cutter moored in the bay. Gus had a brother called Joe who stayed on one of Gerry's tugs. He was dead scared of sharks and never went swimming, but quite often you would see him motoring back to the tug in a small boat, with only an outboard between him and being swept to sea, next stop Columbia, which was precisely what had happened to a guy in Tyrell Bay a few months previously. He had managed to live by drinking rain water until he got picked up, but it can't have been fun. I often thought that Joe was taking a bigger risk than if he swam out there ringing a dinner gong!

Hutch was helping the local kids learn how to sail. They had a bunch of Optimist dinghies that they would use on Saturday morning. Some of the kids would arrive on donkeys. Hutch made sailing canoes that unbolted so he could get them aboard his small yacht. He did a lot of experimentation work on sailing rigs. I talked to him about a rig for my new dinghy. He said, "Come with me and we will get some bamboo for your rig, as I need some as well." This suited me as I also wanted a nice long bamboo to make a spinnaker pole out of. We went off to see a farmer mate of his. We caught a mini bus, and a few miles down the road, it stopped and we got off and walked through the gates of his mate's farm.

It was a small place, but it had a donkey. The farmer showed us around and explained how he was hoping to get more produce from the fields. "It's all down to how much water you have" he explained. Every property had a cistern and some way of catching the rains. Modern cisterns were massive black plastic affairs, but the old ones were made of breeze block and cement. The farmer said that the old kind allowed you to have fish that ate up the mosquito eggs. He took us into the jungle and soon found some good bamboo, he cut it with the machete he had brought for the job, and then helped us carry it back to the road. Hutch made a phone call, and a pickup truck arrived to carry it back to the bay for us. I asked Hutch how much I owed for the Bamboo. He looked puzzled; "Pay?" The whole island seemed to run on favours, I gave him $50 EC anyway to give to the farmer, and he was very happy with that.

Helen took me out to Windward on one of the local buses. These are the main transport on the islands, and they have a motto "always room for two more", they are just ordinary minibuses, but they get crammed full of people sometimes. The fare is 3.5 EC dollars, and from Tyrell you catch the bus into Hillsborough, then you catch the bus to Windward that also cost 3.5 EC dollars. Windward's big attraction was the ship builders. They built local schooners directly on the beach. Simple boats, powered by sail. They used the local woods, and cut the frames and planks out with a chainsaw. You would think that with these basic building techniques the boats would be crude, but no. They could build boats out of wood that even Bloody Mary had trouble beating.

And they were cheap! Leroy told me he could build me a 50 foot schooner without the engine and sails for US$50,000. That's far cheaper than a modern boat, and there were several schooners sailing around with the red duster flying. We went walking and I saw an old man having trouble getting his sheep in the pen, I helped him close the gate, he thanked me and we could not help to notice his accent was very English, he told us that he had just retired from teaching, for most of his career he was teaching Chemistry in Huddersfield. He showed us his house and the house where he and his brothers had been born in. The old house was tiny, empty, but had a view to die for. The other houses around were owned by local families. After more sightseeing we caught the buses back.

One evening I was in the slipway restaurant and I overheard Jerry talking on the phone. A Bavaria 38 yacht had been towed in, the gearbox and engine had seized up and they could not get the engine out of gear. The charterers had left the yacht on one of Jerry's moorings. Jerry said he would find someone to sail it back to True Blue bay in Grenada. I told him Helen and I would do it. He asked what qualifications I had, apart from being able to sail a Ferro cement schooner around without and engine. I told him I had a RYA cruising instructor ticket, to which he replied "Yeah that will do". With that he phoned up the owner and passed the phone over to me. I spoke to the guy, and he asked me how much, we haggled and agreed on $120 American and two tickets so we could return on the Osprey ferry. Helen and I went aboard to get it ready that evening. Jerry said he would help us off the mooring at 08.00 the next morning. I ran about checking the Bavaria to make sure it was all there, and got a mask to dive and check the keel and rudder had no damage. All was okay.

The next morning Jerry came over and helped me get the outboard off the huge RIB and onto the push pit. Then after advising me to keep the single reef I had put in the night before, he stood by, while I raised the main and Helen dropped the mooring ropes. We came off clean and very slowly because the wind was light, cleared the bay. True Blue was only 50 miles away, but we wold have to sail down the lee side of Grenada to get there. As the morning warmed up the wind dropped off. I took out the reef. The fore sail was very small and there was no pole to steady it up with, so we were attempting to broad reach as much as possible to keep the speed up.

The wind came back suddenly and our speed went up to 7-8 knots, but the RIB started surfing down the biggish waves and bashing the transom, Helen took the helm while I shortened up the painter and put fenders out. We were having a great sail, the sun was getting hot and I got rid of my clothes. Our course became more downwind. Helen was down below when an American yacht that was motor sailing crossed just in front of our bows, I had to put the wheel over to miss him and that put us on the edge of a disastrous gibe, we just got past the idiot by the skin of our teeth, I was so cross I forgot I was stark naked as I told them what I thought of them.

After this a squall hit us, Helen was again down below when the wind went up to about a force nine and completely overwhelmed the rudder. The yacht rounded up and headed precariously for the rocks. I steered it into the wind and feathered the main so we slowed down, then the torrential rain hit. I was soon looking like a drowned rat, but the squall passed and the hot sun came back. Helen came up and asked if I had been swimming! We continued our fast progress and were soon approaching our destination. We arrived off the bay and called up for a RIB to tow us in; the entrance is narrow and there was a nasty pile of rocks near, so I thought a tow would be most sensible.

Once we were safely tied up the engineers came on board to try and sort the gearbox. I was amused to see them attempting to gain access to the Morse control. I produced the dipstick to the gear box, which had been subjected to extreme heat and was melted and all curly; "I think it's more serious than that, boys" I said. They put the screws back. Helen and I went ashore and eventually found the boss, we got paid and he gave us our Osprey tickets, then he thanked us for a job well done. I asked him if he had any work, and gave him my card. He told me not just yet and put my card into a stack of others.

We were in time to catch the vomit comet back to Carriacou - it was a very bumpy ride. We caught a taxi back to Tyrell Bay and by 22.00hrs were tucked up in bed on Gloria.

The local buses were good fun; sometimes they took very round about routes depending on who or what they were dropping off. They also delivered small parcels, money, food and petrol. We saw a lot of the island by using them. Most of our shopping was done in Hillsborough and that's were the best internet café was. But the best places to eat were in Tyrell Bay. On Friday nights the calypso band would strike up in the Old Rum shop. There was even a floating bar called the Hallelujah, which was run by a lady called Sally, the better half of Paul O' Reagan who was Gerry's boatyard manager. They owned a huge dog called Paddy, which was perfectly behaved and a good sea dog, as you approached their catamaran paddy would let out a warning bark, a very good dog indeed, he would graciously let people aboard the bar, but he was a very good bouncer!

We soon became good friends with Sally and Paul. When Sally had a problem with her electrics and Paul was too busy I helped out by using my generator and charger to charge Hallelujah's batteries for Don's birthday party. Don had been part of Tyrell Bay for many years; he used to run the boatyard when there was no road access to it. And the slipway was the only possible way for the local trading schooners to be brought out of the water. He had re-invented himself as an architect, and was building fantastic houses for the very rich up in the hills. His problem was getting paid, I was told. He lived on an old Baltic trading ketch that was too big for anyone in Carriacou to lift out, each evening Don would have to start his pumps to clear the bilges.

Helen had run out of holiday and regretfully had to go home. I had originally planned to leave at the end of April but I had been told that the weather would be too bad to cross the Atlantic until at least May. Jerry Stewart also pointed out that Gloria would not be able to point high enough to sail past the islands until the wind stopped blowing from the north east. I also wanted to go as I was running out of money, but if there was one thing I had learnt was not to fight the elements. With a very heavy heart I went with Helen to the airport, waited for a bit before she finally sent me off in the end. I am rubbish at saying goodbye; I always find it extremely upsetting. I made it back to Gloria in time to wave her plane goodbye as it passed over the anchorage.

Helen at the helm

Chapter 22

I had a bad attack of the blues and rowed ashore for a walk, on the way back I stopped at a boat that looked a lot like the one my father had built many years ago. I had heard the owner had crossed the Atlantic more than 40 times. His name was Paul Earling Johnson, and I saw him sitting in his cockpit. He was well into his seventies yet his hair was still blond. Wide shoulders and big arms told of a strong body, but his ankle was a right mess - some months before he had rolled his dinghy in the surf off Hillsborough, his foot had gone through the dinghy and the wood had made a nasty cut. He had been taken to hospital and patched up. Later on he had tried to sleep on a table, not being able to get out to his anchored yacht, but the wind was so strong it had flipped the table onto him, and he had been taken back to hospital!

I pulled up alongside and I asked him if it was true about how many times he had crossed the Atlantic. He said he had only done it 38 times, and then he asked me aboard and poured me a rum with lime juice. He showed me a picture of the 18 foot Shetland boat he first sailed across the Atlantic on, and the hairs went up on the back of my neck. In 1963 I was knee high to a grass hopper, my family and I were on a camping holiday on St Agnes, one of the Scilly Isles. My father had heard there was an interesting man anchored on a small boat by the beach so he went to see him. I wanted to go but could not swim, and as there was no dinghy available swimming was the only option.

So I was taken back to the tent, crying all the way, a man seeing my distress used a biro to draw an anchor on my forearm, and said

"You will be a sailor one day". Later that day my father returned with a wooden sculpture, a head, a bit like the Easter Island heads, he had bought it from the skipper, who was an artist. The picture Paul had just shown me was the boat! I asked him if he had been in the Scillies in the early 60s, "Yes I was" and he did sell a sculpture! The more I talked to Paul the more I realised how much he had influenced my father, and indirectly, me. Paul had branched off into designing boats, the one my father had built being one of his designs.

We talked boats and sailing most of the night. I had a chance to mine a mother lode of knowledge, Paul was well into his seventies, and he had been born on a Colin Archer yacht and spent his whole life in small boats. We discussed many subjects, but the bit I value most was his tips on making Gloria self-steer. That was the one problem with me making a singlehanded passage back to England. Paul said he had a complete Aries wind steering stored up forward " but you don't want that", then he showed me how to make Gloria steer, just using a few blocks, some rope, the staysail boom, and a bit of bungee cord.

Blindingly simple, and as it was the way he steered his own boat, it obviously worked. There was loads of stuff like that, bits of genius, nuggets of wisdom such as how to construct booms out of wood that are just as strong and light as aluminium. The best marine engine, (SAAB), how to make a good dinghy, (he saw mine, and said it was a good first effort!), what the best rum was to drink. By then I was a bit tired and emotional, he might have passed on the secrets of the universe, I would not have remembered!

I woke up on Gloria with a very bad hangover and some crumpled diagrams in my pocket, but it was much later in the day before I was in any condition to get off the boat. I went to the Hallelujah bar and saw Sally who proclaimed that I was suffering from "Male Caribbean island syndrome." Girl gone, man hits the rum, sometime later the wreck is repatriated home!" I said I wasn't but that I had just met Paul Johnson. "Yeah, that's the start" she said.

Jerry Stewart was going off to collect a tug, and would be away for a couple of weeks. In his absence I offered to walk his dogs. His wife Danni said ok, go and get them. I went to their house, let myself into their yard, and the dogs launched themselves at me. Luckily they were friendly, Shadow was a big black sort of Labrador, and Nina was some kind mongrel. They loved a long walk and for the rest of my stay I hardly missed a morning walking them around the bay. I and the dogs enjoyed the walks so much that even when Jerry came back I was there to pick them up at 06.30 each morning.

They had behaviour problems, in the past they had attacked a couple of goats and killed a cat, most of the time they were fine but you could not let them off the leash because if they saw something they could kill, they would be off. I found this out once to my cost. I had got them to the point where they would come back to me if I let them off, then one morning I was throwing sticks for them into the sea, they were having fun, and then Shadow heard a goat in the woods, and that was it! They just whizzed off, I followed and caught up with them as they cornered a goat in the yacht club, shadow had it by the neck, on the ground and was choking it, I kicked him off, and got the leash back on. At that point I turned around and Jerry, Shadow's owner, and Trevor the goat's owner were looking at me from the yacht club veranda! Fortunately

149

the goat shook its head and trotted off, none the worst for its ordeal, and I learnt I could not trust Shadow and Nina off the lead.

I still thought I could leave earlier than the sailing guides had said was the best time. A yacht I had not seen came in called Gaucho. She had the air of a real lady; double ended beamy, a bow sprit that went on forever, two masts made of varnished pine, and about 45 foot in length. I rowed past and stopped to talk to a man doing some wood work in the cockpit. He asked me aboard and that's when I first met Dennis White. He was a slight man with a damaged right hand. I could tell he was American as soon as he spoke, he told me he lived in Martha's Vineyard. I looked at the exquisite job he was just finishing off. He asked me about Gloria which was anchored just astern of Gaucho. I told him my story and mentioned that I wanted to sail back soon. He said "If you do, it will just take you longer, because you will lose your sails, and maybe your masts, and even your boat, wait until the end of May at least". His casual matter of fact way of talking was far more shocking than anything else he could have done.

Then he told me about how he had just lost his yacht last November. His friend and his friend's daughter left Martha's Vineyard with a North West wind forecasted. Their destination was the Caribbean, by way of Bermuda. But the wind went north east, and blew hard. The Gulf Stream running at 3 -4 knots into this wind made huge breaking waves, one of these caught them and smashed the coach roof, rolled the yacht and dismasted them. The boat rolled upright, but his friend had been caught in the wreckage of the mizzen mast and dragged overboard. His friend was dying, and although Dennis managed to get a hand on him, he could not stop him from being dragged away, his friend asked him to let him go.

There was no time to mourn. The man's poor daughter and Dennis had a stark choice, pump or drown. They pumped but the sea came in just as fast as it went out, and after three days and nights of pumping the level of water in the boat had hardly reduced. Then Dennis managed to get a wooden patch on the worst of the damage and at last the pumps made. The decks had been swept clean of any spars, or poles except for a dinghy sailing rig, that had miraculously stayed on board. Dennis rigged this and to their amazement and joy, the little scrap of sail gave them a speed of 2 knots, they were 200 miles from Bermuda, but now they had a chance. The next day a container ship came close enough to see their flares, and 6 hours later they were rescued, but Dennis's beautiful self-built ketch was lost.

After talking with Dennis, I decided that I would follow his advice as he certainly knew first-hand what he was talking about. Speedy John and Ronnie his wife, the owners of Gaucho came back. They have owned her for 25 years and brought up a family aboard her, but now she was too big for their needs. They loved her far too much to sell her and I could see their point. Gaucho was built of an Argentina type of Greenheart; all the planking was as hard as iron. The whole vessel had an air of no nonsense practicality.

Down below the theme continued. The bunks were more like small cabins; the chart table was just the right size. The table was slung on gimbals that some engineer had designed. The only thing I did not like was the fact that she needed more than 8 foot of water to float. Dennis was also a master of sheet to tiller steering and had got her steering herself on the trip down to Carriacou... What a wonderful yacht that I was sure would take you anywhere. Speedy John told me they had come to Carriacou to haul out and do some maintenance and then they would move out of the hurricane area. He and his wife had been in the Caribbean for more than thirty years; they knew everybody and were good people to talk to.

I think it was the day after I was having a bite to eat on Gloria when a Canadian yacht came in, and attempted to anchor. The skipper had a very strange technique; he came in fast, dumped his anchor and loads of rope warp and then motored through the still sinking rope. Well of course it got wrapped around the prop, stalled the engine, and he came to rest just in front of the reef. The skipper clocked that things had not gone to plan and his yacht was pointing a different way from all the other yachts. He got his RIB into the water shouted lots at the woman on board and attempted to push the bow of his yacht into the wind. I watched this performance for a while, and then another RIB arrived and also tried to push the bow around, I decided to help, and putting my snorkel gear into my little dinghy rowed over.

I asked the lady in the cockpit for a coil of rope, she could only speak French, the skipper translated and gave his permission, and I attached the rope to a handy mooring buoy, and then rowed back to the yacht. The rope was not quite long enough, so I attached it to my painter, then got hold of the yacht and pulled it until I could attach another rope from the yacht. Once the ropes were joined we could take the weight off the anchor rope. Then I reached the stern and dived down and took the anchor rope off the prop shaft. Job done, I returned to Gloria.

That night I went to slipway, and met up with Jerry, he said "saw you rescuing that yacht today, I was impressed". So I asked him for a job. We talked about my qualifications and it seemed that I would need an American qualification to work on his tugs, so he said he would try and get a mate's ticket on account of the certificates I had. He emailed the powers that be, but eventually the answer came back that I would have to take the appropriate courses to gain an American mates certificate, I had neither the money nor the time to do this.

Helen was worried that I was never going to come back to England; I told her that the weather mid Atlantic was still too horrible to even think of. So she decided to come out and see Gloria and me again. I think maybe she thought I was going to run off with an island lovely, she was only gone for one month in the end, before returning. I was glad to see her back, but the week before she showed up Gloria and I had another adventure.

Chapter 23

It does get windy in Tyrell Bay, but the wind usually comes from the north east, so as long as your anchor is well dug in there is no problem. It might get a bit rolly sometimes, but that's all. The charter boats that come in are skippered by people of various abilities. Some of them are simply not used to anchoring, and some of them are equipped with anchors and ground tackle that's just too light. But most incidents get sorted out with good humour and minimal damage, but on the night of the 6th of April not only had a fair number of charter yachts anchored, but the ARC round the world rally were in Tyrell Bay as well. The place was crowded. And that night the wind got up.

We were very securely anchored with the bower off the starboard bow and the smaller CQR off the port bow. We were rolling about a bit and that plus the noise and heat made it difficult to sleep, but I did eventually get off. At approximately 04.30 I heard the shout I had been dreading, "Ahoy Gloria" I came out the fore hatch that was open like a rocket, there was a 45 foot steel yacht coming sideways towards our port bow. A man was on the fore deck, he shouted " we are dragging, we are going to hit you, and so is he!" he pointed up wind, out of the gloom came a 54 foot Sun Odyssey called "Tzigane", also sideways onto the wind and dragging quite fast. The other yacht "Ventoso" hit us first, I attempted to fend off, the skipper John told me to stay out the way, our I might lose my hands. The boats were bashing together, there had been no time to dress and I was still in my sleeping attire, i.e. nothing, and so was John's wife. We got some fenders down and then Tzigane hit.

At that point I managed to put my foot down the fore hatch, I landed hard on my ribs, the pain woke me up a bit - I needed waking up, because I had started to feel like it was all a bad dream. Tzigane was bashing hard into Gloria's bow sprit, it was only a matter of time before she did some serious damage, but what I was most afraid of was that with two other large yachts all swinging off Gloria's anchors, the chains might part, and I would have not enough time to get sail on before going up on the reef or bashing into another of the anchored yachts behind us.

First priority was to lessen the strain, so I borrowed a torch off John the skipper of Tzigane. Shining it down revealed that Tzigane's keel was caught on Gloria's bower anchor chain, so by carefully slacking it off Tzigane dropped back and came alongside. I managed to get fenders in to stop the damage that was being inflicted; all the time the boats were hitting each other. One slip and I could have easily lost a finger or too. Then the crew of a French yacht arrived. They helped to fend off, while another ARC boat got a kedge anchor out for Tzigane, and once they were stabilised, we turned our attention to Ventoso. The skipper slackened his anchor chain off and he laid behind Gloria, and the French crew took out a kedge for them.

I had a quick word with Ventoso John and asked what had happened. He told me that Tzigane had dragged into them, then attempting to free their anchor had dragged Ventoso off her anchor, and after some frenzied full speed ahead in the crowded pitch black anchorage, Tzigane had shut his engine down and both yachts had dragged into Gloria. "Well there does not look to be too much damage" I said, going below to get some clothes on, count my fingers and have a well-earned cup of tea!

156

At first light I put my scuba gear on and went down to sort out the tangled anchors. I took my anchor chain off Tzigane's keel, and then checked for damage; apart from some scuffed gel coat there was not any, but I could not but notice that Tzigane's anodes had all but wasted away. Then I found his anchor and lifted it over the chain it was caught in, surfacing I spoke to John and said "Right you're clear, there is no damage to your yacht but you need to replace your anodes", he said "ok I am off then", I did not want to stress John out any more than he was so I simply said "What about some money then" he said "okay I will sort some out".

At that point I presumed that he meant he would re anchor in the bay so we could sort out the damage to Gloria and Ventoso, and I did not want to be around his prop when he left, and because of my aching ribs and knee I did not want to get out of the water, so I just held onto Gloria's stern ladder until Tzigane left. Because of this I did not witness or take part in the exchange between Ventoso John and Tzigane John.

After I sorted Ventoso's anchor out I came up. Gus arrived with Dr Pepper and helped us in the final stages. At last when it was all done and I looked around for Tzigane. "He's gone" John said. "What, gone, gone?" I asked disbelievingly. "Yeah, he gave me $100 dollars EC to give to you!" Janet and John asked me over for breakfast, they went off and re anchored. I went over for some dearly needed sustenance.

I rowed over to Ventoso. Janet had cooked up a good breakfast, and John was joking that it was not often he got up at 4 in the morning and found his wife naked talking to a naked man! We had a good laugh and then talked about Tzigane. I said; "I can't believe

157

he just left like that" to which Janet and John confirmed that they were equally bemused. They had been sailing Ventoso around for 12 years and Janet said "never at any time have we been treated like that". Just after she said that I saw Tzigane entering the bay. I said "see he had second thoughts and returned to sort things out". We watched as they attempted to anchor, they seemed to be having so much trouble I rowed out to see if they needed help.

I asked John if he wanted my help "Yes please" he said. I tied my dinghy up to his sugar scoop and climbed aboard, John introduced me to his wife Jan, and we went into the anchorage to find a space. Several problems became apparent; John was not used to handling Tzigane in confined waters with a strong wind blowing. He kept letting the bows blow off, and once the wind got hold of the bow it was gone. Also Tzigane was such a big yacht his poor wife was too far away to easily communicate with, by the time John had selected a spot and Jan got the message to get the chain out Tzigane had blown off station. There was simply not enough space for that kind of messing around and matters were made worst by the fact that according to John, the chain counter was broken, so they did not know how much chain they were putting out.

Fortunately another ARC yacht was leaving a mooring and he called up John to ask if he wanted it. I suggested to John that he go and help his wife and I would put Tzigane on the mooring. We did this without incident, and after we were safely moored up I spoke to John and said "Ventoso has some damage to his pulpit and some stanchions, and you and I need to have a conversation as well". John said "We are in a real rush just now; we have to go to Hillsborough to clear out, because we have to go to a wedding. I will come and see you when we have finished in Hillsborough". It's easy to be wise after the event, at the time I thought they were nice people who were just a bit stressed out after a nightmare of a night, so I agreed to this.

I went back to Ventoso and drank several cups of tea. Janet and John are easy people to like, so time passed quite quickly, indeed, we were having such a good laugh, I failed to see John and Jan emerge in their RIB from the dinghy dock, Ventoso John spotted them first, "Is that them?", he queried. "No can't be, they would come over here to see you" I said. But it was them, they boarded Tzigane lifted their RIB and dropped their mooring, and then shot out of the bay like the hounds of hell were after them!

I borrowed the VHF and called them up on channel 16. Tzigane answered, and I asked them were they were going. John replied; "We have a wedding to go to, as there is no damage to either of your yachts I am going." I could not believe what I was hearing. I told him there was damage to both Ventoso and Gloria, and that he should return immediately. He flatly refused to. Janet called him up as well and told him to return and sort the mess out but her request also fell on deaf ears. He came up with some cock and bull story about Ventoso dropping their anchor over their gear, which was blatantly not possible because Ventoso was anchored at least 400 metres behind Tzigane, and this verified by several witnesses. I called him up and said that whatever it took I would be following up what I thought was despicable behaviour. He was obviously not going to stop and I did not trust myself not to start swearing at him over the radio so I stopped talking to him.

Janet wrote a letter to the Caribbean Compass paper about the incident and so did I, although they would not print the name of the yacht there was only one Sun Odyssey 54 in the round the world ARC, so all his posh friends must realise what a horrid specimen he is. Later I hauled in my anchor and found that one of the flukes was bent on the bower and the 10mm chain was stretched and kept jumping out of the gypsy, the nylon anchor rode on the port side anchor was chaffed and damaged. The replacement costs for the damage done was £800. I found out John and Jan Underwood's address and sent them the bill, not surprisingly I have had no reply as yet. However, I have sent them a free copy of this book.

Chapter 24

Gloria came through the ordeal very well, all things considered. There was some cosmetic damage but she was not very tidy in the first place and I realised we had got off lightly. A few days after this drama Helen arrived!

She came up from Grenada on the Osprey ferry and I met her on the dock. It was so good to see her again unexpectedly before my return to the UK. We got a taxi back and went to the slipway restaurant to see everybody before wobbling off to Gloria much, much later.

I told Helen about the problems we had with the expensive yacht that was dragging and she was very sympathetic to Gloria, walked around inspecting her wounds! A couple of days later we had a rerun! The wind got up again, another dark stormy night; of course I could not sleep, and kept getting up to check things out. Finally in the wee small hours I got off, Helen woke me at 04.00 as she got out of bed, I came up. "What's wrong" I enquired. "I don't now, but something is not right." I had a look on deck, I could not see much as the rain kept slashing down, the wind was howling and we were getting blown about, but the anchors were well dug in and holding. I was just about to get back into bed when Helen heard a foghorn. I went out and saw something silhouetted by a spotlight. A nightmare! There was always an old trading schooner moored well in the bay. She was owned by a couple of local guys who used her as a storehouse for the wine they sold to the yachts. She was about 65 foot long, and was made from local wood, fastened with mild steel nails, and when she was built some fifty years or so previously she had been built as a schooner. In fact she was the last vessel of any size built in Tyrell Bay. Her grand days were far behind her - now she only had a foremast and a large deck house, the paint had peeled from her hull, and from the frequent pumping I surmised she leaked badly. Now to my horror I could see that she was on the move, coming through the anchorage, and that we could well be in her path. With no engine we would be a sitting duck, if she hit us we could be knocked off our anchors and end up wrecked on the reef.

There are always choices. I could have stayed on board Gloria, and maybe we would have been safe. I could have called for help on the radio, but did we have time? There was another course of action available; I could board the runaway and anchor it, or get the engine going. I told Helen I was going, "put some clothes on this time, and be bloody careful"! Wearing shorts and a T-shirt, I boarded our small dinghy, which seemed to have shrunk. I carefully warmed up the motor as the last thing I needed was to be swept to sea with a flooded engine. Once it was running smoothly I cast off, and told Helen to get on the radio and call up some help. The runaway was much closer; it just got past a catamaran. I got alongside and carefully climbed up a fender and tied off the painter with double knots, I switched on my flashlight and had a quick look around, it was not good.

There were several old 12 volt batteries littered around, an old generator lay on its side by the wheel house, inside another Honda generator looked more promising, but a look in the engine room dashed all hope of getting the engine started , oily bilge water was already lapping over the deck boards and the engine's lower belt pulley wheels. We were being blown down on a Danish ketch, I shouted to them to get out of the way, "We cannot, our anchor chain is jammed" the skipper called back, " Start your engine and go astern" I told him, which they did and were able to just scoot out the way, we went past with inches to spare.

I got up on the foredeck and found a small anchor, it had about fifty foot of chain attached, we were in about 20 foot of water, so it was not enough, but perhaps it would slow us down and buy us time. As it stood, if we did not hit anything, we would be blown out to sea, not a happy prospect. The anchor bit and I managed to get a couple of turns and a hitch on the old mooring rope that was hanging off the bows. Then we were getting close to an American yacht, I shouted at them to get clear, an American female called back that they were there first! I said," this things going up on the reef, if you don't get out the way, it's going to take you with it! "

Then their bow hit my dinghy, the outboard was knocked off and dropped into the sea! I pulled in the dinghy and thankfully the rope to the outboard was made off, pulling on this I was able to recover the outboard, and lie it down in the dinghy, but I knew it would not run until it was stripped and cleaned, and for sure I would not be able to row against that wind so I was now stranded. Fortunately Helen had all the time been shouting for help on the radio, blowing foghorns and waving spotlights, the anchorage was by then very much awake!

The first to arrive was John, Jerry's brother; he put the bow of his RIB against the American yacht and pushed them clear. Then Chris Simmons showed up - he is off a yacht called "Percussion" and as well as being an outstanding musician is also a Vietnam vet. As he came alongside I said "morning Chris, coming aboard?" He replied

"Well I was just going to go ahead and try and clear the way, but, what the hell," and he climbed up, then Mark Oppe and John climbed aboard, and at last we had a crew!

John and Mark got busy rigging a tow line, while Chris and I backed up the anchor chain I had put out with a coil of rope I found. Just as we let about 80 foot of rope out, she started to softly bump, although it was dark still, I could hear the sea breaking on the reef, I knew we were very close to it. Just then Paul O' Reagan showed up in his rib, as he is the boatyard manager and had access to the small but powerful workboat "Dr Pepper". I was even more that usually glad to see him! "It's a job for Dr Pepper", he said, "Will she hold while we get her?" "I think she will, but hurry up" I said, and he went off to get Gus the very talented local skipper of the work boat.

I was able to get the Honda generator started and connected up a bilge pump and started getting the water out of the engine room, but after 20 minutes or so it started pumping oil out so I stopped it. Two things then happened; the first was that one of the owners Popo came on board. While he was running around shouting a lot, the dawn arrived, and we could at last see just how close to the reef we were. Popo shouted louder but no-one could understand much of what he was saying. Gus arrived with Dr Pepper, Mark and John helped rig the tow, and I got Popo to use his massive strength to pull in the anchor. As the work boat took the strain, the anchor came in with one of its flukes bent over. Then Popo said he wanted to go inside the reef, a manoeuvre I could only see as completely impossible, I told him so, and since we had no radio that worked aboard then he should address his request to Gus in person. Popo stormed off and even ran his dinghy over the towline on his way to see Gus!

Although we moved at first, we were still bumping on the sand, the old boat was at 90 degrees to the wind but Dr Pepper could not pull the bow through the wind. I expected at any moment to feel the unmistakable crunch of hard coral under the keel. John and Mark were even using their RIBs to help Dr Pepper get more grip, but even that was not giving us enough to get her free of the sand's clutches. I had a brainwave, hanked onto the forestay was a big old scruffy sail, I found a halyard and bent it on. Chris, reading my mind said, "You're not?" I said "Sure am, find me something for a sheet!" he said, "I'm a Vietnam vet, so this is nothing!" he found another old lump of rope we used for a sheet, then hoisted sail and sheeted in. The pull from that old sail was incredible; she just surged forward and came right off the sand! Then Paul and Gus started making signals that we should drop it, because now we were towing Dr Pepper to sea! The rain came down again and we got another good soaking as we went past Gloria, I waved at Helen, she was very happy to see us all in one piece although she was also soaked to the skin.

Gus shortened up the tow and I heard him and Popo discussing what mooring to put the boat on. Popo was pointing to a half sunk buoy , Gus said; "You really are as stupid as you look, you just broke off of one old mooring you never check, now you want me to put you on another? Well you can fuck off, I will put you on that one and that's it!" So he put us on a big ships mooring, and once safely tied up we started getting ready to leave. Popo came on board and tried to get Gus to come on, but Gus was really cross by then and would not talk to him. Popo pleaded; "but you've got to show me how to start the generator so I can pump out", I gave him a look, turned the switch, pulled the cord and it fired up. "We have been up for hours, getting soaking wet, saving your boat and stopping it wrecking other yachts, and all you have done is shout at us. You have even said thanks" I told him. As we were getting off he handed us a bottle of wine each and mumbled something. Gus took my dinghy in tow and I climbed aboard Dr Pepper for a lift out to Gloria. As we left I noticed that the bilge pump I had started up was now pumping oily water directly into Popo's dinghy. Gus and I exchanged sniggers like naughty schoolchildren but failed to draw Popo's attention to this impending catastrophe.

Chapter 25

Back on board Gloria, Helen gave me a hero's welcome and a good breakfast, but I did not get much of a rest because a yacht came in with a rope around its prop, requiring my scuba services. It anchored near us, and I climbed into my scuba gear and went off to cut it free. The skipper's wife rowed over and paid me $100 EC for doing this, so I used it to treat Helen to a good meal in the slipway restaurant that night. The following morning the skipper of the Danish ketch brought over a bottle of wine and thanked me for helping him get clear of the runaway.

Helen had another month to spend with me on Gloria, and what a perfect month it was; we had made some really good friends, the temperature was perfect, and we had still not yet seen the entire island so we went for long walks and bus rides exploring. Each morning I would still walk the dogs. Slowly we were fitting in, and we loved it. When the royal wedding between Prince William and Kate was broadcasted we were asked by Fitzroy if we wanted to watch it with him and his boyfriend at his house just behind the slipway restaurant. We came ashore at 04.30hrs and I escorted Helen across the sand past the crab holes, into Fitzroy's garden, past the huge but docile Rottweiler dogs and to this door, he was glad to see us, I left Helen there and went off to get Mary, an American lady, who wanted to watch it too.

Once we were all assembled we had a fantastic time. Fitzroy was a wonderful host and kept the tea and bacon butties coming. Helen and Fitzroy had a common passion for gardening and spent ages in Fitzroy's garden talking plants. That was just one of the days that stood out - we always seemed to be doing something. Sometimes we would eat on someone else's yacht, or sometimes we would host a dinner party. Gloria is roomy below, comfortable and a great place for chewing the fat. Helen was able to see the inside of several well-travelled yachts and speak to people who had been living this way for years, and slowly she began to see that it could be a wonderful way of spending some years.

I read in the pilot book that there was a very good engineer in Tyrell Bay whose name was Ouvey. I asked Jerry about him and he confirmed that Ouvey was the man. I left a message with Jerry asking Ouvey to get in touch as I wanted to fix my engine if possible. The problem was that it was such a big lump it would be difficult to get it out. By then I suspected that the oil pump was the problem, and to fix it we would have to get the sump off. In due course Ouvey showed up and arranged for the lifting equipment we needed.

I disconnected everything and we lifted it. This sounds easy, but believe me it wasn't! After a couple of hours we had it suspended from the coach roof, we got the bolts of the sump out, and then the sump itself, and the problem was exposed. The bracket that held the oil pump on had snapped. The oil pump had gradually moved away from the gear that drove it, and taken out the feed pipe while it was doing so. Ouvey looked closely at it and then gravely pronounced his verdict; "The gears are damaged, the bracket is cast and cannot be welded. To fix this engine you will need a new pump, and then you will need to strip the crankshaft bearings to make sure there is no damage."

This was obviously impossible given the time frame and my financial position. So we lowered it back in its hole and I put a strap over it and did my best to forget it.

On evening I was cooking a chicken curry that Helen and I were going to eat while we waited to see if we would get a green flash as the sun went down. A gaff cutter came in under motor, as there was absolutely no wind. The skipper took it out of gear and as the way came off and she glided to a stop the skipper casually walked to the bow and dropped the anchor. The manoeuvre was carried out so competently I turned to Helen and proclaimed; "That guy really knows what he is doing, I have to meet him". I had cooked far more dinner than we needed so I rowed over and asked the man if he would like to eat with us. He said "Sure", and came over with a bottle of wine.

The name of the boat rang a bell in my head - it was called "Iron Bark". He introduced himself as Trevor Robertson. Over dinner I realised we were entertaining a legend! Trevor and his wife Annie Hill were awarded the American cruising club medal in 2009 for a voyage during which Trevor single-handed down to the Antarctic, and spend the 8 month winter frozen in, then sailed out picked up Annie after which they went to the Artic and spent another winter frozen there! All without any outside support! He was fascinating to talk too - another font of wisdom. His boat was so well organized, really clean and well painted.

He called on us a day or so later and invited us for drinks with a few other people. The other guests were Paul Johnson, and the French Skipper accompanied by his lovely girlfriend, of the 100 year old Zulu Leenanhead. Probably more experience and knowhow between Trevor and those guys, than in the whole of England. It was a fascinating evening, and I was particularly impressed by the determination that Paul showed in attempting to lure the French girl from her boyfriend, and the copious amount of rum he drank!

I had met a man called Pete Evans while Helen was away. He had what can only be described as the perfect job; he was the paid skipper of a large ketch owned by an elderly lady called Pat, who employed him to sail her about. Most of the time was spent in Tyrell Bay, where Pete kept his own yacht Richonate. In the afternoons Pat would send Pete off to play after about 14.00 hrs. Once he found out that I had dive bottles aboard Gloria and I wanted to go diving, most afternoons he would show up with a big RIB and we would go diving. He knew the area very well and was a very good diver. We soon started diving the more unspoilt reefs and dive sites. Peter had a habit of tweaking the tails of anything dangerous. The first time this penchant for annoying the local wildlife surfaced was when we met a stonefish. We pointed at it and made the cutting throat sign to each other so we both knew how poisonous it was, and then he got hold of its tail and waved it me!!

The next day we dived the Brother's reef, it's offshore and strong currents sweep past. Pete found a large nurse shark's tail hanging out of a cave; he just had to tweak it. The shark shot into the cave, but emerged from another cave very close to me. It was extremely cross, and although I pointed at Pete and tried to tell it that he was the disrespectful one, I could see that I was likely to get bitten if I did not move away slowly!

One time on the Brother's reef Pete went in first and I had a problem with a strap, so by the time I made it down to the sea bed Pete was not in sight. I thought we were going around anti-clock wise. I went off to look for him. When I got into the current I turned around to find a large Barracuda looking at me, with his mates all behind him like a lager lout on a Saturday night itching for a fight with the comfort of backup in close proximity. I swam towards it, thinking that showing fear might bring about an attack, but the barracuda held its ground. I backed off and swam back to where the RIB was anchored. I finally met up with Pete there and we had a good dive until my air started getting low. Pete used very little air, about half of what I would use, but we could manage a 60 minute dive most days, after which we would race back to get the bottles refilled for the next day. After talking to Pete about my father and step mum, he realised that he not only knew them, but had been at their leaving do when they had left Trinidad all those year ago!

The man in the dive shop got the raving hump because we were diving lots and he was only getting a few dollars to refill our bottles. The reality was that he wanted hundreds of dollars off us to be our guide, so matters came to a head with Pete having a blazing row with him. Fortunately there was another place we could get our bottles filled up so we could still dive most days. Once we explored some sunken ships, the first of which was empty. The second had occupants in its wheelhouse, under the watch chair was the biggest lobster I have ever seen, big because he had a mate with him that stopped anyone wanting to come in the wheelhouse, his mate was the biggest Barracuda Pete or I had ever seen! We left them to it - that was one fish that Pete did not tweak the tail of! Helen started referring to Pete as my wife as we were spending that much time together.

The last dive we did went a bit wrong for me - a typical case of complacency making a situation dangerous, which played out as follows; John Baptise was the local pizza parlour owner, who, as you might have guessed by the name was French. Very French. He had dived with Pete before and John was astonished to find out that he had used more air on the dive than Pete. John Baptise was going to dive with us on the Brother's. That morning I was not feeling very well and chucked up my breakfast. I went back to bed after that and I should have stayed there that day, but when Helen called out "it's the wife" I got up and went about getting my gear sorted.

John Baptise made space for me and I climbed into the RIB. Pete and I would usually do a circuit of the reef and find out which way the current was running, then moor the RIB to the down current mooring, this meant that the first part of the dive we would swimming against the current, then we would get swept back to the rib at the end of the dive. John Baptise did not like this because it meant that on the last part of the dive we would be going deeper, so we did it the opposite way.

From the start I felt uncomfortable; I could not slow my breathing down and was sucking great lungful's in and using up my air rapidly. It did get a bit better, still I knew I should have bailed out straight away, but every moment I delayed the current swept me further from the mooring. At last we were on the far side of the reef, and started swimming towards the other side, we met the current, and checking my air I realised I did not have enough to make it, so I swam over to Pete, showed him my gauge and made signs. He made the swimming sign. We only had a short way to go to get out of the current and we attempted to make it but a little time later we hit a wall of water, I had to swim really hard and the effort simply used up too much air and suddenly I sucked dry! I swam over to Pete and showed him I was out of air, we were at 16 metres and I knew that a panic here would kill me. Pete knew it too and made the calm down sign. I was not having a panic attack, but I knew that if I did not get up to the surface soon I would not have enough oxygen in my blood to make a slow assent, so I was a little anxious.

Once Pete was convinced I was not about to rip his regulator off him he handed me his second regulator and we made a controlled slow assent. On the surface we had to swim really hard to get out of the current, and I was disturbed by the thought that we were right in the area where the Barracuda hung out! When we got into the shelter of the rocks Pete told me to swim and hang off the mooring while he went and found John Baptise and picked up the RIB, then they would come back and get me.

While I hung onto the mooring I had time to reflect. I knew I was responsible for my predicament and it was certainly my own fault, but what was making me really uncomfortable was that I had to rely on other people. I had had to rely on Pete for air, and now I had to rely on Pete and John Baptise to make it back to the RIB, then come and get me. If they did not make it, then I would struggle to make it back to the RIB myself, and I certainly would not be able to swim back to the island. To my relief I soon saw the RIB with Pete and John Baptise coming to get me. I expected to get a hard time from them about my stupidity, but John Baptise had to admit that he had almost no air left by the time he got back to the RIB. As usual Pete had loads left, God knows what he breaths down there, but it's not air!

Chapter 26

Our time was almost spent by then; Helen had to again reluctantly return. I was very nervous at the thought of a non-stop 4500 mile trip, through the cold and gale ripped waters of the North Atlantic, single handed, with no autopilot, no engine, and no long range transmitter; I was going to be truly on my own. Jerry asked me if I needed a life raft. I said no, but I could use a SSB receiving radio, which he had and gave it to me. I brought it back to Gloria, after the ritual morning dog walk. Helen greeted me, not with the usual cup of tea but with the worrying statement "I can hear water running, but I can't see where it's coming from. Down below the bilges were filling up, which I pumped clear with the big double action bilge pump.

The water was coming in from a place near the main mast compression post. I put on a mask and slipped over the side, the first place I went to was the fault in the keel. I had noticed a flaw halfway between the Canaries and the Cape Verdes. It had never leaked, and it did not go very deep. But now I put my hand in and a fish swam out! I swam up got out told Helen to keep pumping and went ashore. The first person I met was Paul O' Reagan. "You look a bit stressed Max." "Yeah the boats sinking" I replied. He looked at me, and knew I was not joking. And although it was a complete pain in the ass for him he said "Okay we will get you out now, Gus will tow you in" I was so relieved, I could have kissed him!

Gus showed up and towed us in, the big lifting rig got us out in short order, and hoisted Gloria high in the air, Jerry was there, he looked at the hole, put his hand up inside, his fingers came out covered in mud, he sniffed it "that's Essex mud, you have been kept afloat all this time with Essex mud!" My legs went a little wobbly. Gus came over and advised me to stay in Carriacou; he even said he had another engine I could have. His argument was that once a concrete yacht starts falling apart they don't stop. But I saw it differently, I did not know why a lump had fallen out of the keel, but it had happened a long time ago and the rest of the hull appeared solid, so all we had to do was repair the hole. Once Gloria was jet washed off, and blocked up Jerry came over and we discussed how to fix the problem, Jerry phoned a civil engineer he knew and was told that a 3 to 1 sand/cement mix would be best, and throw some caustic soda in the mix as well.

Another call got the cement on the way. I had seen a big pile of sand near the entrance of the boat yard, and said I would go and get a bucket full. Jerry looked at me like I was an idiot, "No, leave it to me". He made another call and got Fitzroy to get the sand - it seems that a visitor helping himself to sand is a no-no, but it was okay for Fitz to do it! All the ingredients arrived the first day, and Gus lent me a huge drill and a hole cutter. With the drill I cut an inch hole in the compression post, and then I filled the cavity in the keel with reinforcing bar and welding mesh. Under the cavity I rigged a piece of plywood to block the bottom then I made a nice sloppy mix of concrete and with a funnel, poured it into the compression post, 4.5 gallons later the post was full, and so to was the cavity. While Gloria was out I also took off the prop and anti-fouled. I got a shock when I bought the antifoul, the cheapest stuff I could get still cost $100 (U.S.) for a U.S. gallon (smaller than an imperial one)!! I needed two gallons to get around, but she did look good.

Before we could get Gloria back in, Helen had to go home. We spent the last night together on Gloria in the yard, and it was horrid! Mosquitoes were in abundance, and even though they could not get through our mozzy net the whine they made kept us awake. It was so hot and airless that it was a less than an ideal last night together, and we had to get up really early to meet the taxi driven by Linky in the morning. We arrived at the pier to wait for the Osprey ferry but it was too upsetting for me and I could not wait there. One last hug and kiss, I told her I loved her and walked off. I wanted to walk back to Tyrell Bay, but a jeep stopped and offered me a lift which was so like Carriacou. So with a heavy heart I arrived back at the boatyard.

The concrete had set and I was able to tell Paul we could go back in. He was visibly pleased because our emergency had thrown his schedule - for getting hurricane storage yachts out - all to hell. The lifting rig dropped Gloria back into the water that afternoon. We stayed a night by the harbour wall to check that there was no leak, and thankfully it was completely watertight. I went in to pay the bill. I wanted to put it on my credit card but the machine would not accept it. Back on Gloria I scraped all the cash I had and just had enough together to cover the bill. I had a little bit for provisions to cover the long trip home, but that was it. I went to slipway to report the good news about the ex-leak to Jerry and Paul.

Jerry was concerned. "Are you really going to do it, he asked?" I said "Yeah, if you don't think I will make it, let's have a little wager!" His reply was a bit off putting "no, because if I win, you'll probably be dead and I won't get paid!" I could not fault his logic, but I still didn't like it! Jerry told me that the wind would go south east for a few days starting on the 13th of May (a Friday) and then it would rain hard for a week. This window would give me enough time to clear the Windward Islands and get enough sea room to be able to make northing enough to eventually reach the westerly winds somewhere north of Bermuda. That would give me a day to restock, although I did not need much time as I had a lot of dried food aboard, and anyway I did not have an abundance of money to buy much. The boatyard bill had just about cleaned me out, for some reason my credit card had been declined, and I could only pay the bill by scraping around and finding all our emergency stashes of cash.

However I did not like the idea of starting such a trip on Friday the 13th. I took the outboard off and stowed it away on the pushpit, and then rowed into the beach and caught a minibus into town. I was able to buy a monster tin box of crackers and some veggies, and a few tins of corned beef. To ward off the bad luck of leaving on a Friday 13th I bought a bag of limes off an old lady who sold stuff on the pavement, the price was $5.00 EC, I gave her a $50.00 EC note and told her to keep the change " God will go with you " she said, and I think it was $50. 00 well spent.(indeed apart from the valuable blessing, those limes lasted for six weeks!). Rowing out to Gloria I stopped to have a last word with Paul Johnson. Ronnie and speedy John were aboard, but I passed up the offered rum for a glass of wine. Paul went over the best route for me, and showed me his chart with the last three trips that way he had done, his advice was priceless. "Go the best course north you can, without going further west than 60 degrees west, keep going until you get to 38 degrees north then you can head towards Flores, or if you want, go straight to England, just don't cut the corner" and speedy cut in and said "I heard of a guy with no engine, cut the corner and a few months later they found him, dead, run out of water. You got enough water Max?" I thanked them for their advice, reassured them I had plenty of water and left. I rowed over and said goodbye to Hutch over a coffee, and he wished me well. I saw Chris and Linda from Percussion, they invited me out for a meal later and I went and said some more goodbyes. So many friendly faces to see, yet I missed a lot of people. If I had to do them all I don't think I would have left, because it was becoming too painful to say farewell to all those fine friends.

That night in the Slipway Chris and Linda treated me to a fine meal, and too much booze. We went back to their yacht and had a singsong, drank even more and Chris gave me a crate of beer as a parting gift before I rowed away to grab a few hours' sleep before dawn. In the morning I walked the dogs for the last time, said goodbye to Jerry, and rowed out to get ready for the big off. Speedy John came over to help get the sails up, there was a light easterly wind, and this made it easy for me. I pulled up the CQR anchor and stowed the rope, then hoisted the jib, the staysail and then the main staysail, Gloria paid off on the starboard tack, and we were away, I sailed up to Percussion and Chris took some photos. Then we were gone.

Chapter 27

Rounding the headland past the Sisters Rocks I rigged the rope to tiller self-steering. It worked beautifully and Gloria was sailing herself, leaving me to tidy up and have lunch and put the trolling lines out. The sailing was wonderful, Gloria was moving along with a lovely motion, eating up the miles at a steady 6 knots, her clean bottom and no prop helped no end. Soon Carriacou lay well astern and we were passing Union Island. That night I snatched an hour of sleep while we crept up the lee of St Vincent. The next day was spent getting clear of St Lucia and the wonderful wind finally left us between Martinique and Dominica. At first it fell light and then there was nothing at all.

We were only about three cables (six hundred yards) from the rocks of Martinique, and still the water was too deep to anchor, but 12 hours later the wind finally came back and we made our escape. The course we could make was not as good as before but it still would allow us to clear the islands, so we kept going. I could not relax because we were still too close to land. I called up Helen when I got a signal and told her that there was not much in between us except 4500 miles, and that she should not worry if she did not hear from me for 8 weeks or so. I called my Mum and then my Dad. Then I put the phone away, knowing that it would shortly be nothing more than a paperweight anyway.

The fishing line went tight, I pulled it in and there was a 35 pound Wahoo on then end. After successfully landing it I cut the head off, getting rid of those nasty looking teeth. I filleted it and put aside enough for a good meal, and then I salted the rest. My father nearly died some years ago in Trinidad, He ate a Wahoo and went into anaphylactic shock. He was taken to hospital in a truck, bleeding from his eyes. The driver had turned to my step mum and said "Your man, he gonna die", so I was a little hesitant to eat the first mouthful when I cooked it, but the taste was something else and I must own up to pigging out on it!

The rest of the fish after salting was dried in the sun, and kept for the rest of the trip. I found that the best way to eat it was to cut up a small chunk and add it to some noodles. It made a delicious lunch. My diet was nutritious but a little on the bland side. I had enough porridge to last for about 6 weeks, but not much of other cereals. I had not bought any eggs as I had found that the eggs we bought in the islands did not last very long, so there was little point in buying many. But I had loads of bread mix and flour. I started making "plum duff" using currants and brown sugar, with a drop of olive oil to provide the fat, and this was surprisingly tasty. Most dinners consisted of veggie stew with several different pulses in it; I would put the pulses, chick peas, barley, lentils, chunks of "soya meat substitute" and dried peas, in to soak overnight, and then cook them in the pressure cooker for about twenty minutes until they were soft. Then I would cut up a few onions, open a large tin of tomatoes and throw it all in, a few Oxo cubes, a bit of pepper, boil it up with a tin of veggies, and that would keep me going for about four evening meals. When it got totally boring I would add curry powder.

We made fantastic progress the first few days and Gloria stunned me by reeling off 135 miles one 24 hour period. The sailing was wonderful, with 7 knots at times showing on the GPS. I began to think that we might make a really quick passage, but the wind went more north easterly and our course became hard on the wind. The sails I had up then were the working jib, the stay sail, the main staysail and the main with 4 rolls in it. This plan balanced Gloria out really well, but I began to be concerned about the working jib - although it had started the trip in good condition it was made of lighter cloth than the other sails and would probably not take too much abuse.

I had another sail of about the same size but the foot was too low, so I re cut it and sewed a new clew into it. This project took a few days, but I was pleased with the result and hoisted it while I started to over haul the light working jib, just in time because the seams had started to go. As we got into the horse latitudes the wind went lighter. On occasions we would get a total calm, during one of these I went for a swim, there were no fish, no nothing, just an endless blue.

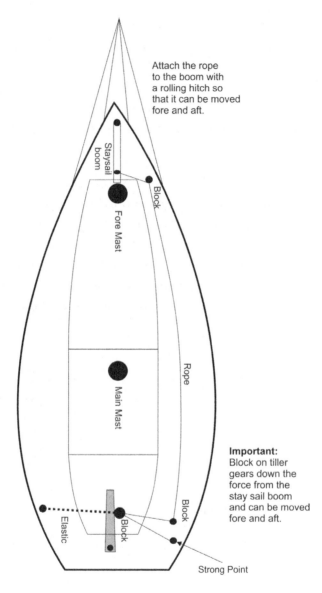

Attach the rope to the boom with a rolling hitch so that it can be moved fore and aft.

Staysail boom

Block

Fore Mast

Rope

Main Mast

Important:
Block on tiller gears down the force from the stay sail boom and can be moved fore and aft.

Block

Elastic

Block

Strong Point

Tillar to Sheet Self-steering for Gloria

Chapter 28

Sometimes I would be able to get the fisherman sail up. This delightful sail was a big square shape that went between the mast tops. It was very good in light winds, but I would always take it down at dusk - we were beginning to get hit by squalls and it could be catastrophic to get clobbered with that sail up. It was a pig to get down as well, and quite often it would get caught and then I would have another repair to do on it. Life was very busy for me. I would snatch an hour or so of sleep, but there always seemed to be something that needed fixing, or a sail change or adjustment to the steering that needed to be done. I also had the SSB receiving radio to play with. Paul had given me the frequencies for the American weather forecast, but it was some kind of robot and very difficult to understand. This radio also had AM on it and I could pick up lots of American stations, but mostly these seemed to be Christian evangelical stuff that got tedious very rapidly and had me more likely to question if there is a God rather than reaffirming my faith in Him.

The Sony reader Helen had given me now came into its own, she had filled it with hundreds of books so I had plenty to read, but sleep was my biggest problem. Even when I did get my head down I seemed to be half awake, which was good in one way as when the wind shifted I was very rapidly on deck to sort things out. But I soon began to feel the effects of long term sleep deprivation, the most noticeable thing was that I always felt there were other people on board, at times I found myself putting two cups out when I made tea.

The most time I had ever spent alone had been the four day trip between Porto Santos and Grand Canaria. Now after a period of weeks I found myself getting very emotional about insignificant things. I began to dwell more and more on my past life, the mistakes I had made seemed to become of greater magnitude than they had assumed before. I began to despise myself, and this went on for at least a week. Then one morning I had a moment of clarity - one of those realisations that make a big difference. I really got the fact that what had been done before was done, I could live a better life in the future and in the now, and gradually I calmed down and won the victory of feeling comfortable with myself and able to be by myself. It was a magic moment, and I think seldom experienced by many people today.

Our course became more north by west. I really wanted to go north east but the only way we could go was towards New York, we started to get close to Bermuda. If I had an engine or crew I would have gone in there, but as it was I gave it a miss - I had no money and plenty of food, and after a particularly savage rain storm, our water tanks were full.

Once we were about 150 miles north of Bermuda and after sailing for 3 weeks the wind got a bit of west in it, and at last we could point towards the UK. We were on our way! The next day we ran into another calm. I had grown to accepting the calms and as I baked in the sun I saw a massive turtle. I took photos of it, it swam up and I identified it as a loggerhead, it started scraping its shell against Gloria's keel. A small shoal of fish came with it. After a while more fish came along, followed by a bunch of dorados. Out of the corner of my eye I kept seeing black shapes surfacing. I managed to hook a big dorado on a lure; it shook its head a few times, and then went completely berserk!

It was leaping, tail walking and whipping its head from side to side, it threw the lure eventually and I almost got hooked myself because it hit the boom right alongside my head with a loud thwack! A full on feeding frenzy started, those back shapes surfacing were giant tuna. They started erupting out the sea, the dorados joined in the slaughter with 30 knot dashes that threw up bow waves! As fast as it started it was over and things calmed down, then a wind came and we sailed away. The dorados stayed with us that night and I shone the torch on them. Either side of Gloria's bow they spread out like out riders, escorting a queen. I know they were just making use of Gloria as a stalking horse; the flying fish would take to the air when she got close, and the dorados would be waiting when they landed, but it seemed more magical than that. More like Valkyries bringing a fallen warrior to the halls of Valhalla, to feast with Odin, all I needed was a bit of Wagner to listen to and I would have been convinced.

That night it got cold enough that I had to put on some clothes, and the next day the dorados were gone, as was the aquamarine colour to the sea, it was starting to go grey, but Gloria was in the groove and romping towards home, and she had found the blessed Gulf Stream with its 2-3 knots of favourable current. I could not complain. I saw a whale breach in the distance, I was glad it was a long way off, 70 foot of whale erupting for most of his length vertically makes one hell of a splash when it goes back in!

I began to see whales quite frequently. I think they thought Gloria was one of them, she was travelling about the right speed and the black antifoul looked very whale like. I also started to be able to pick up Herb the famous weather router on the SSB radio. He was sending the yachts closest to me back down to Latitude 35, into light and variable winds, which is okay if you got a motor and plenty of diesel but no good for us. The first really bad blow started up and I struggled to get sail off and get Gloria steering on course. I just about had it sorted, when we fell off a wave and all the electrics went off. There was only 30 minutes before night fall, and I had nothing - no lights or navigation instruments.

Leaving Gloria to herself I dashed below. I knew there was a common negative connection on the engine; my first thought was that it had come off; I reached under the engine to check it and found that it was arcing out!!! I managed to get it disconnected and then put a multi-metre on the engine; I found that the engine was showing 12.65 volts! I expected any moment to have to deal with a fire; nothing I did seemed to make any difference to the current in the engine. I got out a pair of snips in the end and cut the whole wiring loom. That did it.

Then I started re wiring the boat. Lights first, then the navigation and so on. It was a good job Gloria knew which way to go. We were getting bashed about a bit but when I did get topside, we were on course and doing 7 knots, so I left well alone and went to try and get some food and rest. The wind kept blowing. 24 hours later I thought it freshened, but when I checked the GPS we were only doing 5.5 knots. I was really tired and put the discrepancy down to my exhaustion, and went below to try and rest. At first light I noticed a long orange sea monster following the boat!

Once a bit of common sense crept into my thinking I had a good look at the monster and realised there was something around the skeg. The wind dropped down and I was able to hook up the "monster" It was a long lost life raft drogue and rope. It had been in the sea a long time, and there were goose barnacles growing on it. The rope was all tangled up. The drogue had been working effectively, and was a real sod to get aboard. I realised that the wind had got up the night before and we had gone through the lot of it with far more sail than we should have had up.

I was having trouble hearing Herb properly but I thought he said that after the strong blow we had had the wind would go N.W. for a few days , then go back to SW and blow again, which is exactly what happened. We slowed up and at least I got a bit of rest, but on 19th June I heard Herb telling a yacht called Bear To get the hell north above lat 42 as fast as possible because of the bad winds that were due, we were at lat 41, so what was the choice? Go south and prolong the blow or go north and hope? We went north and 24 hours later the wind started to howl.

I was reducing the sail, the barometer was dropping fast, the waves were getting real big, but the thing that was making life very nasty was a swell that was running at an angle to the swell driven by the wind. Our speed was making a big wake and this in turn was making the big waves break. But I needed to find a way to get Gloria to steer herself and slow down; Gloria was on the point of broaching. I was rapidly running out of energy. I started letting ropes out over the stern, as each one reached its end, I tied another to it, once I had all the ropes out I tied off the tiller and went forward to drop the sails, and I was hoping the drag astern would keep her running before the wind. It did at first, but then a massive wave loomed out of the darkness and she just turned into it, I had not clipped on, and was in between the two masts on the lee side, as the wall of water reared up I realised I had screwed up badly and I was going to pay, when we went horizontal I would be washed overboard.

But it did not happen, good old Gloria assumed a nice lean, then because she was 14 foot wide but only drew 5 foot 7 inches she was pushed sideways, I saw the huge pressure wave building up like a bow wave on the lee side, hardly any wave even came aboard, but a lump of concrete capping rail landed at my foot! I got the sails down, the ropes were keeping Gloria slightly off the wind, so it seemed to me that the safest course of action was to shut up the companion way and stay below. And that's what I did, as big waves came thundering in and hit us, heralded by a sound like a steam train, every now and then. The water found every weak spot and soon the whole inside was running wet, but apart from filling up the cockpit and getting past the companionway boards, the waves did not do a lot of damage, or so I thought.

About four hours later, I felt the wind easing, Climbing out I got my first sight of the massive swell that was running, but the wind had definitely dropped down a notch or two. I put up the working jib and the stay sail, once the sheet was made off to the tiller and Gloria was steering herself I started to recover the trailing ropes. I got a few feet in, then we dropped down a wave, the rope ran out and I stupidly tried to stop it, at which point it very nearly dragged me over.

It took an awful lot of work to get the ropes in. I was sweating and my muscles were on fire by the time the cockpit was filled up with what seemed like miles and miles of the stuff. I set too coiling it all down and stowing it. My right arm was aching and it felt like I had pulled a muscle in it, it needed resting, some chance! I got some sleep, maybe a couple of hours, coming up I saw the staysail drop to the deck. The inner forestay had gone. This was really bad news, because I needed the staysail to steer.

The mast fitting had pulled out. I had to repair it, and looking around the spares locker I found a short bit of rigging wire with an eye at each end - it was just long enough to go around the mast twice. I routed around until I found a handful of shackles, then sorted out my bosun's chair. This was connected to a four-part tackle. My next problem was my arm with its pulled muscles had to do even more work and if the rolling boat bashed me against the mast and I lost my grip, there was no one to help me. I waited for daylight, and then it was time. I got up there fast, the repair worked well and less than an hour later we were back under sail and Gloria was once more steering herself, I went below for a cup of tea. It tasted horrid; I checked that water, definitely a salty taste to it. I unscrewed the deck filler, the o ring had failed, and sea water had got in.

Using some PTFE tape I sealed the deck fitting, at least I had two fresh water jerry cans lashed to the deck, I went and checked them, both had been smashed by the waves. This left me the water in the emergency tank, about six gallons, a 5 gallon jerry can and another small 5 litre spring water container. However the brackish water could be used for cooking so I only needed the fresh water for tea. I heard later that we had come through a gale with storm force winds, The North Atlantic was certainly living up to its rep!

Dorado on the hook

Chapter 29

The hard weather and lack of sleep, constant work of changing sails, reefing and fixing things was taking its toll. I looked in the mirror, and an old man looked back. But we made progress and one day we were at last less than 1000 miles from the Lizard. I had promised to be back in England for Helen's birthday, which was the 13th July. We had nearly three weeks to go, so we should get there easily as we were averaging about 650 miles per week. One thing that was slowing us down was that in light winds I had stopped setting the fisherman sail. The last time I had used it at first it had wrapped itself around the top of the foremast, I had to sprint up to the top and get it off before it ripped itself up terminally. The shrouds and spreaders had skinned my bare legs nicely. Then when I had got it up it jammed and I could not get it down. The wind had blown up and Gloria became almost uncontrollable until finally it had gibed and freed itself. I felt the bit of speed we did get from it in quiet weather was not worth the risk associated with its use, so it stayed in its bag below. Every night I plotted our position on the chart, and most nights I saw that we had covered about eighty miles. Our progress was slow but relentless, all I had to do was keep Gloria in one piece and she would do the rest. I no longer felt like the skipper; Gloria was in charge, and I was just a maintenance man!

I was making dinner when I heard the squeaks of whales. I went topsides but could not see anything. Down below again and the squeaking had increased. Back above, and there they were, pilot whales, loads of them, swimming past within touching distance. The herd must have been in the hundreds because they just kept coming past for at least an hour. This must have been some kind of whale highway, because the next day I saw a pod of sperm whales swimming the opposite way, then a day or so later a massive whale kept pace with us and blew 4 times, each time it breathed in I heard a loud "whee" - it was easily twice as big as Gloria, and I was glad it was in a good mood.

Then suddenly we were nearly home. I picked up radio 4 and was able to get a weather forecast. It gave great weather except for sea area Fitzroy, which of course was where we were; another gale on its way. We made progress and then the signal got stronger and the winds lighter, it even warmed up. Then just as we crossed the continental shelf the wind that had become north east failed completely.

It came back fitfully and our pace dropped off to a crawl, it dropped down to twenty miles for a 24 hour day, so close, I could almost smell the land. The next day was a flat calm; I found it almost unbelievable that the sea could be so flat. The next day was the same; fulmars swam slowly around the boat. They looked so hungry I started fishing, the mackerel were biting and easy to catch, so I had them for breakfast and I fed the hungry fulmars. The sun beat down and I was enjoying myself, considering a swim, but then a black fin cut the water and I realised we were attracting the wrong sort of attention.

A French trawler appeared and made a bee line for us, I was getting worried but at last minute it veered off and I waved at the crew, they waved back. Another boat also followed this course, it was good to see people, but I was not sad when finally the wind came back, first from the north east, and then veering to go to the south before freshening from the south west. We were moving and on course. The next afternoon, the visibility was going and rain was starting to fall, but through a rift in the greyness I caught a glimpse of the Scilly isles. I looked at my phone and I had a signal! I called up Helen. It was so good to hear her voice; she was crying and I was too. I had to make it a quick call because my mother and father would be desperate for news, so I phoned them next.

The wind came on and soon we had the best part of a gale blowing us in, overnight we cleared the Lizard and approached the Manacles, I dropped the main I wanted to get into Falmouth during the morning in day light, so I slowed us down to 3 to 4 knots. There was so much traffic around as well as rocks within 3-4 miles so I had little sleep, just cat naps. I called customs and told them I was entering Falmouth from Carriacou in the Caribbean. After giving all my details to the man on the other end of the line he thanked me for my time and told me I had fulfilled all the requirements for entering the country, and I recall thinking "that was too easy!"

During one of the quieter moments

Chapter 30

Daylight found us rapidly approaching Falmouth with the wind gusting up to gale force at times. I wanted to be able to control Gloria when we came in to anchor, so I dropped the main staysail and hoisted the main but deeply reefed to the cross trees; under this rig Gloria was controllable in the big gusts, but had a tendency to lee helm when the wind dropped down, I approached the anchorage; not good as it was on a lee shore, and there was quite a few vessels anchored there already. There were alternatives on my chart, but in real life it looked like moorings had been put in and there was little space to anchor. At least if we dragged it would be into deeper water. I got things ready, brought her up into the wind, dropped the head sails, and the anchor, I had missed a lashing and it took me a minute or so to get the anchor free, by the time it was down we had moved a bit more out into the fairway than I wanted to be, but what the hell, we were stopped!

I pulled the main down and rolled it away, then I saw a black RIB with several crew also dressed in black coming towards me, I was not really surprised, "Customs, may we come aboard" was the request, like I could say no! "Yes you can, but I am going to have a cup of tea" I told them and I went and put the kettle on. There was about five of them; they did not want tea but wanted answers. I did my best, but like I told them, I had not had a lot of sleep in the last two months and none really for the past thirty six hours, so I was a bit slow. Gloria was not looking her best, over the passage a lot of sea water had got inside and things like the wood burner and my tools were rusty, most other things were just plain wet. There were rust streaks down the hull, my hair was a tad unruly and I had a beard Captain Haddock would have been proud of!

The customs were okay, they had a good search, but were not nasty and even sent for another couple of litres of fresh water when I mentioned I was short. Eventually after finding nothing one of the guys asked were the water tank was. I showed them but also said that I had no sealer to reseal it if they opened it, I showed them the entry in the log from when the Portuguese customs had searched us, he read it and said "Well you will be glad to know that Gloria is still a customs magnet babe" quoting what Helen had written all those months ago.

They didn't bother opening it and left soon after, I was humbled to find that the one who had been searching in the fore cabin had made a good job of tidying it up. It was a lot better than when he started! As soon as they left the harbour master approached, his opening gambit being "You can't anchor there". The wind was still screaming and I patiently explained that my engine was not working and I was single handed, and that if I tried to re-anchor in the prevailing conditions I would most likely damage other vessels and could even run aground. "You can't anchor there" was his reply.

How I missed the Caribbean just then. If the same scenario was playing out there, a smiling local would have at that point offered to tow me for $20 EC to a better place, not this po-faced jobsworth. I told him I had not slept in a long time, and I was going to bed, and I would move tomorrow. He left, not a happy bunny. I dug around and found a cigar I had been saving, I smoked it and tried to accept that we had done it; Gloria and I had crossed the Atlantic, 4500 miles all by ourselves, with no engine, no fancy steering gear and minimal electrics.

I would have liked to go ashore but there was going to be no shore leave for me. I called my brother Matt and arranged to meet him in Caw Sands the next afternoon. Then after a meal I went to sleep; a deep, deep dreamless sleep.

When I awoke at 05.00 I felt refreshed. The wind had dropped down and the tide was on the last of the ebb, so it was a good time to leave., I started getting Gloria ready, the harbourmaster was already up even at that early time, close by in his small launch, watching me, after getting up the staysail I hauled up the anchor, we turned downwind and I got the jib and the main staysail up, as we passed the harbourmaster I resisted the temptation to make the finger sign at him.

Gloria slowly passed Black Rock and met the swell of the open sea, which felt more normal than the flat motionless water in the anchorage. Soon we were bowling along at 5 to 6 knots, having a wonderful sail. Gloria liked the course, a broad reach, and as steering was taken care of for me, I had a good breakfast of the bread and plum duff I had baked the day before. The Cornish land was stunning. I passed the places I used to know all those years ago - Dodman point, Mevergissy, Foy, Looe Island, and then at last Rame Head, with the old chapel on the headland, at the foot of those rocks I had fished as a boy. It was the most wonderful sail, the sun was even out and it was a perfect summer's day. As we rounded Penlee Point we came into the lee of the land, but still found enough tide and wind to make a slow but stately progress into Caw Sands Bay. In twenty foot of clear water I dropped our anchor.

I phoned my brother and he came down to meet me. I got the dinghy that Helen and I had built off the coach roof and launched very quickly, then rowed ashore. I set foot on the beach as my brother walked down and we hugged. I took him out to Gloria and we had a beer. I asked him if he could make me an outboard bracket, he took a few measurements and said, "Sure, anything else you need?" I said I was short of gas, and he asked what bottle size. I showed him the Calor 7 kg I had, "No problem." I took him ashore, and we went for a beer in the pub. He had to go back to his metal fabrication business and do some more work, but after showing me where the shop was we arranged to meet the next day when my mother would also be there.

My mother came over on the ferry from the Barbican in Plymouth the next day. I gave her a big hug, and she took me to lunch in a pub where I could see Gloria swinging to her hook. It seemed so unreal, so dream-like, a world apart from the oceans desert to eating with my mother in a beautiful village pub. I savoured each mouthful, and hung on to each of my mother's words. We went to another pub for a beer and to wait for another brother of mine. Toby arrived about the same time as Matt made it back, and he brought with him the finished outboard bracket, a great bit of workmanship. He also had a full Calor gas bottle for me and would take no money for any of it. We went out and put the bracket on. It only took a half hour and fitted perfectly. Back to the pub we had a good time. They all had to go after a while and I stayed to wait for my sister Anna, she was going to arrive with her boyfriend Geoff. To kill time I asked the barmaid if any of the fishermen I used to know still lived in the village, but the only trouble was I only knew their nick names. Chopper she did know, he was banned from all the pubs as he had a bad alcohol problem. Fanny, well he was a Millbrook man, so she did not see him much. I did not mention Buster, because I knew he was dead, took down with the old Pee Jee Angie (a beam trawler) off Start Point in the early 80s. I had worked on that boat with him, and had only left it months before it turned over and sank.

I was glad when Anna showed up. Geoff had brought his guitar, and Anna put her wonderful voice to use and sang my blues away, apart from "In the early morning rain" that made my eyes wet and brought a lump to my throat. Later that night I dragged the dinghy into the surf and rowed back. It had been a stunning day, and so very wonderful to meet up with family.

Chapter 31

Early on Friday morning I got Gloria underway for the Solent. It was slow going at first. Off the Mewstone I failed to see a fishing buoy until too late. It started to follow us but fortunately it did not catch up on anything and gave up the pursuit not long after. The breeze filled in and Gloria began to romp. We were being slowly overhauled by a few yachts, they finally caught us up at Start Point, but I was proud of this. One of the yachts was a bit bigger than Gloria, and it just showed how well Gloria was now going in that she was almost as quick as bigger yachts. As Start Point slid past I worked out a course to Portland Bill. I decided to go well outside the race. Gloria agreed and I let her get on with it. I even managed to get a little sleep.

Daylight found us clear of the Bill. We had had a fantastic sail but now the wind started to fail. Eventually we became becalmed. I shipped the outboard onto its bracket so I could make sure we did not get swept past the Needles channel by the tide. The wind came back but this time from North West. Gloria was revelling and powering along lovely. I phoned up Edmund and he called me back. As luck would have it he was out on his yacht with his wife, having competed in the two-handed Round the Island race the day before. They were in Cowes getting diesel, and he said they would come out and take photos. And then they were there; Gloria was steering herself, downwind, she was doing a good 7 knots with the tide, and Teresa shouted out, "Do you know how fast you're going?" I don't know who was more surprised Ed or me. Gloria certainly seemed to be showing off. I told Ed I was heading for Hardway sailing club. I needed a pontoon berth to give Gloria a good clean up ready for Helen, who would be joining us for the rest of the trip home.

The wind picked up and when we turned into Portsmouth Harbour to sail up to Hardway the wind headed us, but we could still just hold the course I wanted if I husbanded every last puff. There was a big wind shadow just at the entrance but we were getting through when a white dory with two characters in red aboard put themselves on a collision course with us. The wind picked up and so did our speed, I was getting very concerned that I would run down the dory, so I reluctantly turned away from the wind to starboard to avoid them. "Keep to port" one shouted. Idiots! If they had not been there I would have kept to port! We were hitting 7 knots, and as we passed Hardway I had to shorten sail, not easy because of the congestion. I pulled the main down, but Gloria was still going fast. I took off the jib next, and lost my favourite sunglasses, even though they were on an elastic head band. By the time I had all the sail off we were well up the river from Hardway, and I was pleasantly surprised to find the little outboard would push us against the stiff breeze to allow us to moor up on Hardway's pontoon.

The problem next to be solved was stopping: There was not much room on the pontoon but if I slowed up more than the 2 knots we were doing the wind would shove us off course. Going astern on the outboard was futile, the only course of action was to judge the moment to shut off the motor and leap ashore with a rope to brake her with! My plan worked sort of; a kind man helped to stop Gloria from crushing a dinghy that was inconveniently parked in the way. One of the locals, a girl called Carly recognised Gloria and asked me for some kind of write up of our travels. I sat down and tried but all that came out was a poem, so I gave that to her. It went like this:-

Ode to Hardway sailing club.

Me and Gloria left Hardway club,

Where to next? That's the rub.

We wanted to go to the tropical sun,

But that's a lot of miles too run.

Ushant, La Corunna, Bayonna, and Santos,

But by then the oil pressure was lost.

Onwards to Las Palmas for to pick up hands,

Three guys who would walk West Indies warm sands,

Twelve days to Cape Verdes cos the trades don't blow,

This made poor Gloria look very slow.

And then across the ocean we tried to sail,

Light winds, no engine, like a concrete snail!

St Lucia did eventually hove into sight,

Just in time to meet my Helen's flight.

Together we roamed the Grenadines,

And swam in its warm and turquoise seas.

A true unspoilt paradise,

White beaches, palm trees, and people nice,

Far too soon Helen's time had fled,

Sad tears at the airport were shed.

Just me and Gloria left to cross the wild north Atlantic,

Stay in the cold westerly's-that's the trick,

The sea soon lost its gorgeous sheen,

Turned slate grey, and looked quite mean.

The wind blew hard and caused a giant swell,

I had left a heaven and found a hell!

Seven long weeks all alone,

Oh how I wished for a satellite phone!

It does sound foul, but it was not all bad,

It made me value people, and for that I am glad.

Carly, you asked me why I broke my trip here?

It's not just cos it's cheap and you sell good beer,

It's just that real people in this sad world are rare,

And I know at Hardway I will meet some there.

The end

Gloria's flag looked the worse for wear

Chapter 32

Edmund came around later and we had a few drinks to celebrate Gloria's return to Hardway. During the night we had a visitor. I had left the companion wash boards off, and something landed on my feet while I slept. I woke up sharpish, but whatever it was had gone. I thought it was a cat, but half asleep I was looking at the companionway when a dog stuck its nose around the corner! I put the boards in place and went back to sleep. The next morning I saw the lady who had a dog on board, I asked her if her dog got out at night." No that's the fox you saw" she said. Apparently I was lucky not to lose a shoe or a glove. You don't get problems like that when you anchor!!

The next morning I got on with the big clean up, and then I went for a walk into Gosport town centre. It was something of a luxury to be able to buy what I wanted food wise. I never really noticed what a large choice we have in our supermarkets; things like proper bacon, sausages, granary bread, and chocolate biscuits. I really missed those things in the Caribbean. The bacon we could get out there was very thin and had honey on it that made it too sweet. I also bought Helen some birthday presents and a nice card.

Edmund came back that evening with a couple of students; some very successful people who had sold their business and were going to buy a yacht and go sailing. The husband asked me if I thought they could cross the Atlantic. I must admit to being thrown by the question. I think I answered it the best I could by saying that in a good yacht I did not see why not. After a few drinks they left. Edmund stayed for the night, and claimed his old sea berth. It was just like old days and in the morning I cooked a proper bacon and egg breakfast.

Helen was on the 16.00 Hrs train. I was there to meet her. We had a long hug, and then caught a taxi back to the boat. It was just brilliant to be back with her, and it being her birthday the next day, at midnight I let her open her presents. She loved the zippo lighter I got her. It was pink, and suited her, being unbreakable but feminine - very much like the girl herself! The next day we spent in Gosport and caught the Ferry across to Portsmouth to the Spinnaker Tower. I got a good deal on a laptop and a new mobile with Carphone Warehouse. That night I phoned Simon and Anita of "Talisman" and told them we were in Gosport. Simon said to come over and see them in Cowes. He suggested that we could raft up alongside them and get free mooring for a couple of days. This meant that we would also be able to see Chris and Cathy and I would be able to return the equipment he lent me.

The sail the next day over to Cowes was a stunner. The wind was on the nose a bit so we had to do a few tacks, and we crossed the path of a large race with big yachts flying kites, but I made sure we were on the starboard tack when we went through them and there were no close calls. Helen was impressed at how well Gloria was sailing and we had no trouble getting into the Medina. We were soon creeping up the river to Talismans mooring. Simon was waiting for us, and then I totally messed up coming alongside and clobbered his rudder.

For some stupid reason I decided there was no tide running, but there was. The ebb had just started, so when under just the staysail and jib, we tried to turn across it, Gloria stalled, and stopped turning, fortunately we were going really slowly and Simon is big and strong, and fended us off. Not the best way of impressing anyone though, I felt a complete idiot!

Anita showed up after a while, she had been at work. It had also been her birthday a few days before and Simon had bought her the exact same card I had bought Helen, so how weird was that?! Helen was dead impressed with the diesel cooker/heater on Talisman, as was I. The whole boat was wonderfully dry and warm; the cooker was on 24/7 and ran radiators too. She was a bit less impressed with their soil composting toilet, but I thought it a great idea. It saves another two holes in the hull, no blocked up pipes to struggle and swear at, and it does not smell.

We had dinner with them the first night, and they ate with us the second. During the day we saw Chris and Cathy. It was not the best of times for them because Chris got made redundant from his job in the marina. I gave him back his EPIRB, transformer, and American gas bottle, and apologised for how rusty the gas bottle was.

We wanted to go after three days but the forecast was for lots of wind and rain. The fourth day started the same. My passage plan called for a 07.00 start. I did wake up, but the rain was lashing down and the wind was howling, so I went back to bed. A couple of hours later the rain had stopped and the day had brightened up considerably, but we had lost our tide window. Talking it over with Simon later he suggested leaving in the evening. It was a good call and that's what we did.

Our exit under sail was a much better manoeuvre than our arrival. We singled up on the ropes, pulled up the jib, staysail and main staysail, let go the bow rope and her head blew off, then let go the stern line and we were away. We made slow and steady progress down the river against the tide, and I called up the chain ferry on the VHF and warned them we were on the way and only under sail. They held on for us so we could pass, very decent of them. Then we were out in the Solent. That night we made the Looe channel just before the tide turned foul. It was a windy ride, but the weather was behind us, the stars were out and we were having a good time of it, and by the next morning we were off Beachy Head, but Helen had fallen to the scourge of mal de mere.

I could not blame her, we were getting bounced around a lot, but gosh, we were moving, the GPS was showing 7 knots plus for hours once the tide turned with us. I had an idea about getting into the Thames Estuary that night, but that was not to be as the wind strengthened and the sea got up, and with the shipping around I had to stay on watch. I was getting a tad fatigued. I was also worried about how wild the sea was going to get once the tide turned and we got into a wind over tide situation. The obvious haven was Dover; we were only about 6 miles from it, but the trouble was the tide runs hard off the entrance there, and wind shadows from the harbour walls are also a problem. The pilot book advises to keep one's engine running while entering. By my calculations the tide would be slack in an hour and with the amount of wind we had I felt we could carry our way past the dead bits and safely make the entrance.

I called up Dover port control when we were within 3 miles. I explained we had no engine and would be proceeding to the anchorage. He asked me if I wanted a tow from the harbour tug, I told him "no thanks". The thought of attempting to connect a tow in those seas filled me with not a small amount of dread. The plan went off really well, and we came tearing in, past the towering walls of granite that would have punished any mistakes severely. We lost the wind like I expected but Gloria's 16 tonnes were moving at 6 knots,   so we punched through the dead patch without any trouble.

There was only one yacht anchored already so we had plenty of space to choose from. Helen was up and helping me to sort Gloria out. I put the smaller CQR anchor out, because although the wind was blowing the best part of a gale we were well sheltered and the sea was perfectly flat. Once we were secure a police RIB came out and asked us for our passports. I showed him mine and explained I had had a good going over by customs in Falmouth and Helen had only joined the boat in Gosport. They were okay and went away soon after. Helen was so pleased that the world was not cartwheeling around her anymore she made me the dinner I really needed. Then we got our heads down. Good old Gloria had made the trip from Cowes to Dover in 24 hours. Not bad at all.

Chapter 33

The weather raged all the next day so we stayed put and were grateful for those tall granite walls, but a change was coming and next day's morning brought the sun and mild conditions. We left as soon as the tide would serve and made our way up the coast. We just scraped past the North Foreland and it was decision time. My mother had gone to Battlesbridge to wait for us, but the tides had started to cut. We could maybe cross the Thames Estuary that night, but what then? If the wind stayed in the west we would struggle to get up the Crouch and we had only a few gallons of petrol, so good as it was in flat sea, it was too much of an ask to expect the outboard to push us all the way up the Crouch.

There was only one seaman like choice, and I told Helen that we would be going to Thurrock Yacht Club, picking up a mooring there and waiting for the tides to get better. That way we would be able to make her friend Age's party on the 23rd. We had a good sail up the Kent coast, went inside the Goodwin Sands, outside the Brake Banks. The tide was doing most of the work but the small amount of wind did give us steerage and a bit, so we did get around into the Estuary before the tide turned against us, and then a sea breeze got up and we had a good beam reach that allowed us to make over the young ebb. It finally deserted us by Hook Spit, so we anchored and got some rest.

At 02.00 the tide changed and I hauled in the anchor and we got under way. We were on the "overland" route and there were only inches beneath our keel as we worked towards the deeper water, but the wind (a sad zephyr) was right in our teeth and there was a lot of tacking and not much progress. In fact we only made 12 miles towards Thurrock before the tide was again starting to ebb and we had to anchor again. Later that afternoon we "motor sailed" using the outboard and made another 15 miles and the "haven" of Holehaven. There was a big sign saying "no visitor moorings" and some sort of harbour master in a hut on a pier that had heavy grids protecting the windows and coils of razor wire on the roof. This reminded me of a film called "Fort Apache the Bronx". I did not bother to ask permission but picked up a mooring. We were only 12 miles from Thurrock Yacht Club, one more tide, even if we had no wind would do it. So we got our heads down and waited for the morning.

We left the mooring on the last of the ebb, and had trouble turning Gloria around, the channel is so tight she grounded on the bow before she got around, but the long bamboo pole got us off, and before long we were out in the tide. There was a little wind and we made steady progress up past Mucking, then the forts, Pigtailed Dave from TYC called me up and I told them we would soon be there. The wind filled in and we started to make a decent bow wave, we had all the sails up, including the fisherman, and I think Gloria was a grand sight as finally we rounded the last bend and TYC was revealed.

Someone had even put all the bunting out, it was a fine welcome. We picked up the visitors mooring, and Dave came out with a strange young lady who turned out to be on work experience for the local paper. After we had answered her questions we had a tidy up and went ashore were we met Clare, Helen's daughter. She took us to Helen's house in Basildon, and I slept in a proper bed for the second time in 10 months!

We had to wait a week for the tides to start getting big enough to attempt the upper reaches of the Crouch, but on Saturday the wind forecast was about as perfect as it ever gets for that trip. With light north westerly's giving way to a south wind on Sunday, the tide was a little bit small but enough, so we left. The first tide took us to the Blacktail where we anchored. In the early hours the tide came right and we sailed for the Whittaker, daylight found us in the Crouch.

The outboard had to be used to get us moving fast enough. I had done the trip enough times to know we had to be in Brandy Hole, by high water Burnham. That would give us enough water to get over the shallows and enough time to cover the three miles before the ebb started. We had to hold 4 knots over the ground to get to Brandy Hole, and it was a struggle, because the south wind was more like a south west, and very light.

The morning got hotter and hotter. Past Burnham we even were able to turn off the motor for a short time, but it was back on half an hour later. We saw Richard and Martin Bailey on Beluga II, two of my ex-students. Waves were exchanged, then we saw the old lifeboat that belongs to Helen's mate Johnny, and then I saw Del who had moored up alongside us at Battlesbridge once. I called out a hello. We were in Brandy Hole, bang on schedule, but it was getting very congested as there was some kind of canoe race on. Speed boats towing water skiers whizzed in and out of the moorings that were spread all over the place, and just to add to the chaos crowds of swans swam about. It was murder!

Somehow we got through without any calamities. But we were slowed up by a wind that blew hard right in our teeth, but then we rounded the last difficult turn and the wind became our friend again, so we picked up speed. The shallow water alarm was singing its song warning us of the absence of the floaty stuff. The Battlesbridge granary loomed over the river, and suddenly we were almost there. Rounding the last bend we could see the small crowd of friends and relatives that had gathered to greet us. My uncle Fred had decked out the old bridge in flags, and Roy Hart was standing by with a highly polished brass canon. I quickly dropped the last two sails and stopped the outboard. We glided serenely past Roy and he fired his ordinance. It made an almighty "BANG". Gloria slid majestically into her berth. Helen's son Sam dropped my mooring rope over a post and we were home!!

Postscript

We have been back a few months now and I have had time to reflect on our journey. First of all I must acknowledge all those people who helped, to paraphrase Norman Tebbit; Success has many fathers, unlike failure, that is a complete bastard! There are many ways you can read that; the way I see it is that if you are lucky to have support then anything is possible, and I had huge support.

From my girlfriend Helen, who had never been much in contact with boats or the sea before she started hanging about with me, and yet crossed the Atlantic from Portugal to Porto Santos with me, then cruised the paradise that is the Caribbean. My mother Mary for always loving me. My cousin Jim Gallie for his generosity in the subject of mooring fees, my Aunty Shelagh who over the years has stoked my passion for sea adventures by feeding me a never ending collection of good nautical stories. The great Edmund Whelan who encouraged me and shared the adventure, Captain Blood (Jack Vandenbroele) who came across the Atlantic on the outward trip. Trevor Robertson, Paul Earling Johnson for their advice and sharing their wisdom. Jerry, Paul, Gus and Slow from Tyrell Bay haul out, for all their help. Danni and Kate at the slipway for good food and drink! Sally of the Hallelujah floating bar for more food and drink! Peter Evans for the diving, and probably saving my worthless hide. My father Trevor and my stepmother Ley, for the advice and inspiration. Thurrock Yacht Club for being a club that encourages people to sail. Chris Simmons for his friendship and taking the photo that's on the cover. Finally, Martin Bailey (co-owner of Beluga II), who kindly proof read this book (and added this sentence). There are a lot of people I have missed off the list, but you know who you are and I thank you.

From the voyage I gained many things; a great deal of sailing knowledge, fishing and the salting of fish, but most importantly I learnt to value people for who they are. I realise what a blessing true friendship is. I experienced emotions on steroids throughout the trip – the highs of seeing Helen after extended periods, and the lows of her leaving, suffering the extreme north Atlantic weather and the power and violence of its grey seas. It could well be the stuff of nightmares, but to me it's still beautiful.

As I write this, Gloria is safely moored up in her berth at Battlesbridge. Since writing this book I've fitted another engine and have a list of jobs as long as my arm, but soon I hope to have her sailing again. Where to next? I don't know!

Max Liberson.

Out with the old...

...in with the new. A tight fit!

Appendix 1 – Costs

Below are details of the various costs before and during the trip.

Boat - £1500
Rigging - £150
New mainsail - £1000
Fuel - £450
Starter Motors (2) - £300
Engine repairs (before and during) - £250
Food - £700 (only for the out- going and returning trips)
Marina charges - £350
Haul out and antifoul (in Carriacou) - £450
Sail repairs - £80
Building a new dinghy - £250
Cooking gas - £150
Cruising permits (various locations) - £250 (ranging between £30-50 each)
Bag of cement (most of which is thankfully left over) - £5

Total: £5885

Note: I left out entertainment as this 'expense' would vary from person to person depending on their tastes.

Appendix 2 – Watch Systems

The 'Mother' Watch System

This was Captain Blood's watch system for four people that allowed for one day 'as mother' every fourth day.

	1st day		2nd Day		3rd Day		4th Day	
00-02	Max		Ed		Blood		Jack	
02-04	Ed		Blood		Jack		Blood	
04-06	Jack		Max		Max		Ed	
06-08	Max	BF	Ed	BF	Blood	BF	Jack	BF
08-10	Ed		Blood		Jack		Blood	
10-11	Jack	L	Max	L	Max	L	Ed	L
11-13	Max		Ed		Blood		Jack	
13-14	Ed		Blood		Jack		Blood	
14-16	Jack		Max		Max		Ed	
16-18	Max	D	Ed	D	Blood	D	Jack	D
18-20	Ed		Blood		Jack		Blood	
20-22	Jack		Max		Max		Ed	
22-24	Max		Ed		Blood			
Mother		Blood		Jack		Ed		Max

BF: Breakfast
L: Lunch
D: Dinner

After one of 'the Jacks' left we moved to a three day system:

00-02	Max	Jack	Ed
02-04	Jack	Ed	Max
04-06	Ed	Max	Jack
06-08	Max+ Breakfast	Jack+ Breakfast	Ed+ Breakfast
08-10	Jack	Ed	Max
10-11	Ed+Lunch	Max	Jack
11-13	Max	Jack	Ed
13-14	Jack	Ed	Max
14-16	Ed	Max	Jack
16-18	Max+Dinner	Jack+Dinner	Ed+Dinner
18-20	Jack	Ed	Max
20-22	Ed	Max	Jack
22-24	Max	Jack	Ed

Appendix 3 – Map/Distances/Stoppages

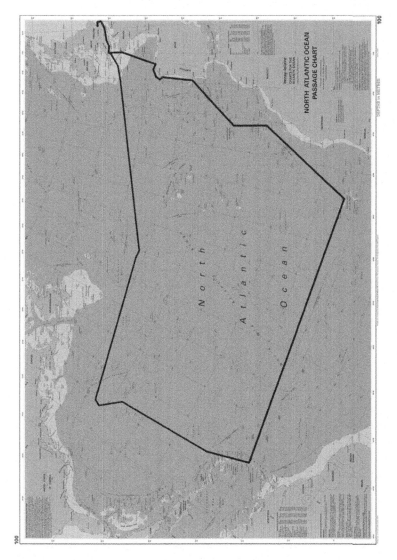

Chart 100 North Atlantic Ocean passage. Chart reproduced by kind permission of Imray Laurie Norie and Wilson Ltd 2012. www.imray.com.

Distances travelled on return leg

From Carriacou to Falmouth, starting 13th May 2011.

Date	Miles	Total	Date	Miles	Total
14/5	96	96	10/6	90	2145
15/5	55	151	11/6	60	2205
16/5	43	194	12/6	111	2311
17/5	102	296	13/6	122	2438
18/5	135	431	14/6	110	2548
19/5	115	546	15/6	110	2658
20/5	110	656	16/6	99	2757
21/5	88	744	17/6	90	2847
22/5	42	786	18/6	100	2947
23/5	70	856	19/6	83	3030
24/5	86	942	20/6	90	3130
25/5	30	972	21/6	46	3176
26/5	30	1002	22/6	103	3279
27/5	74	1076	23/6	102	3381
28/5	90	1166	24/6	120	3501
29/5	108	1274	25/6	87	3588
30/5	100	1374	26/6	104	3698
31/5	75	1449	27/6	104	3802
1/6	21	1470	28/6	107	3909
2/6	40	1510	29/6	98	4007
3/6	90	1600	30/6	90	4097
4/6	60	1660	1/7	31	4128
5/6	75	1735	2/7	52	4180
6/6	70	1805	3/7	16	4196
7/6	85	1890	4/7	43	4239
8/6	80	1970	5/7	116	4355
9/6	85	2055	6/7	77	4434

We arrived at Falmouth after 55 days, averaging 82 miles per day.

Details of stoppages for the entire journey

Battlesbridge, Essex	Depart 6 September 2010
Hardway sailing club	Arrive 9th September
Isle of Wight	Depart 17th September
Ushant, France	Arrive 20th September
Ushant	Depart 21st September
Riada Cedeia	Arrive 25th September
Riada Cedeia	Depart 30th September
La Curruna	Arrive 30th September
La Curruna	Depart 10th October
Lexas	Arrive 11th October
Lexas	Depart 12th October
Finestere	Arrive 12th October
Finestere	Depart 13th October
Oporto	Arrive 16th October
Oporto	Depart 17th October
Penchie	Arrive 18th October
Penchie	Depart 19th October
Porto Santos	Arrive 26th October
Porto Santos	Depart 4th November
Los Palmas	Arrive 7th November
Los Palmas	Depart 19th November
Mindello	Arrive 4th December
Mindello	Depart 9th December
St Lucia	Arrive 6th January 2011
St Lucia	Depart 12th January
Bequai	Arrive 13th January
Bequai	Depart 23rd January
Carouan	Arrive 23rd January
Carouan	Depart 24th January
Mayreau	Arrive 24th January
Mayreau	Depart 28th January

Union	Arrive 28th January
Union	Depart 9th January
Carriacou	Arrive 9th January
Carriacou	Depart 13th May - return journey
Falmouth	Arrive 6th July
Falmouth	Depart 7th July

Note: Some short stops not documented between Falmouth and Battlesbridge on return leg.

Battlesbridge	Arrive 31st July 2011.

Made in the USA
Monee, IL
21 May 2021

69177785R00128